LOCOMOTION PAPERS          NUMBER ON[E]

# THE
# LEEDS NEW LINE
## THE HEATON LODGE
## AND WORTLEY RAILWAY

by
Roy Waring

THE OAKWOOD PRESS

© Oakwood Press 1989

ISBN 0 85361 369 9

Typeset by Gem Publishing Company, Brightwell, Wallingford, Oxfordshire.

Printed by S & S Press, Radley, Oxfordshire.

All rights reserved. No part of this book may be reproduced or transmitted in any form or by any means, electronic or mechanical, including photo-copying, recording or by any information storage and retrieval system, without permission from the Publisher in writing.

# Acknowledgements

This work would have been totally impossible without the friendly help and co-operation of many individuals, and institutional organizations, who have made generous contributions. To these people I tender my warmest thanks and it is only appropriate that their names should be recorded.

D.K. Atkinson, A.S. Bagot, R. Brook, R.E. Caws, G.S. Cooper, P. Crockford, P.T. Disbrey, K. Evans, J. Fisher, G.B. Goldthorp, R. Hardy, G. Hesp, D. Hird, J.H. Hirst & Co., G. Hogg, D. Holmes, M. Jennings, Kirklees Libraries & Museums Service, L. Layton, City of Leeds Library Service, Lens of Sutton, N. Marsh, J. Mitchell, National Railway Museum, E. Pilkington, Real Photographs Co., Public Record Office, F. Robinson, West Yorkshire Archive Library, N. Walker.

Also to Peter E. Baughan for his very generous friendship and help.

Published by
The OAKWOOD PRESS
P.O.Box 122, Headington, Oxford.

# Contents

|  |  | |
|---|---|---|
| | Introduction | 5 |
| Chapter 1 | Conception and Planning | 7 |
| Chapter 2 | Construction of the Line | 15 |
| Chapter 3 | The Route Described | 27 |
| Chapter 4 | The Early Years | 51 |
| Chapter 5 | After Nationalization | 73 |
| Appendix | Working Arrangements | 93 |

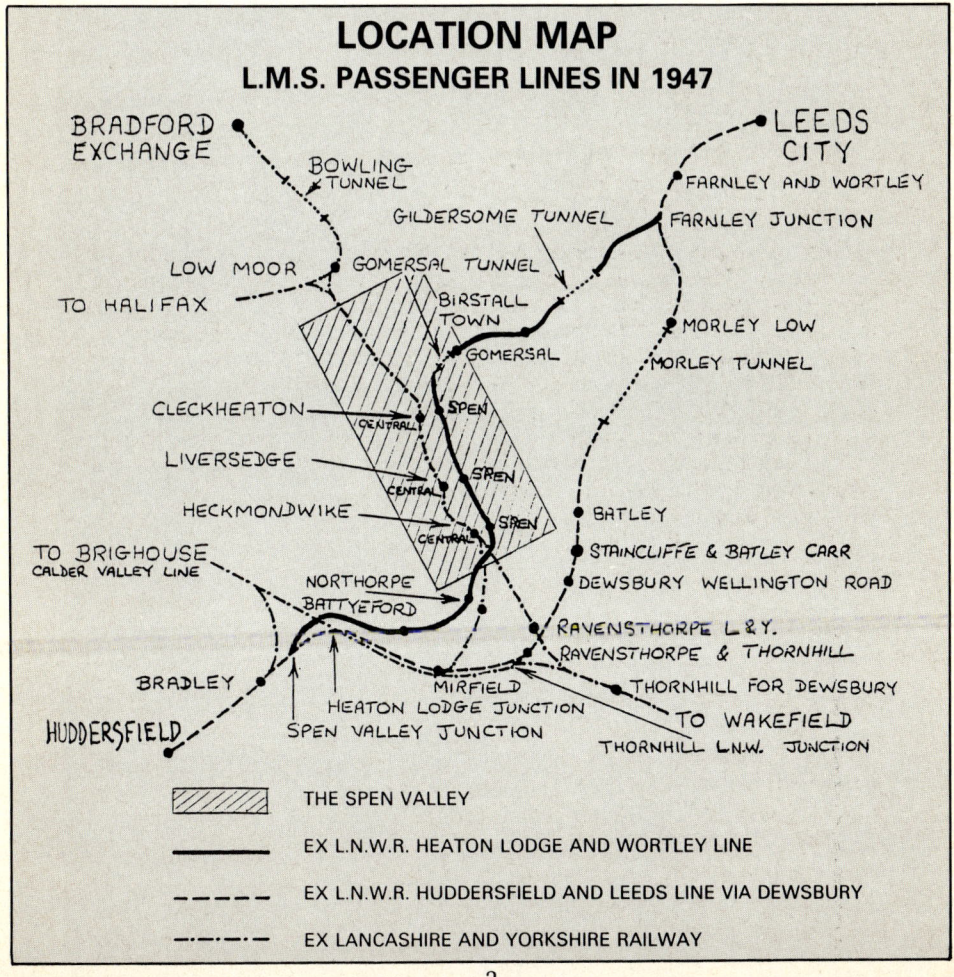

## LOCATION MAP
### L.M.S. PASSENGER LINES IN 1947

Littletown (c.1905) looking across the valley towards the Heaton Lodge and Wortley Railway with Liversedge station in the distance. *Photograph Courtesy of M. Rathmell*

# Introduction

You may ask, why write about this relatively unknown railway? Well, this is really the story about the railway of my childhood when I lived in Heckmondwike, but more so because it includes the history and the life of the "Heaton Lodge and Wortley" Railway. During construction, the line became well known to many people as the "Leeds New Line" and this nickname has remained with it throughout its life and even to this day, more than 20 years after its demise, although at the time of closure British Railways was calling it the Spen Valley Line. For these reasons the book covers the line in its entirety, with emphasis on the Spen Valley.

The Spen Valley gets its name from a tributary of the River Calder which flows down the valley and is known as the River Spen, although local people affectionately call it the Spen Beck. The towns in the valley are Heckmondwike, Cleckheaton and the district of Liversedge which comprises a number of small towns such as Hightown, Roberttown, Littletown and a few more.

In 1915 Liversedge, Cleckheaton and Gomersal were formed into the Spenborough Urban District but Heckmondwike remained a separate community having its own Urban District Council. Things remained like this until 1955 when the Spenborough Urban District was created a Municipal Borough, this remained so until 1974 when all these places were merged into the newly created Kirklees Metropolitan Council, based at Huddersfield.

In 1848, the Lancashire and Yorkshire Railway Company constructed a line down the centre of the valley to run between Low Moor and Mirfield, so when the London and North Western also decided to serve the area as well, its railway had to cling to the east side of the valley.

By the year 1900 the Midland Railway Company was also considering building a line down the Spen Valley from Bradford. This was to enter the top of the valley at Oakenshaw and pass along Cleckheaton Bottoms under the LNWR viaduct, then down the valley through Liversedge and Heckmondwike, before heading off towards Dewsbury. The Midland Railway Company promoted a Bill in 1898 to construct the line from Royston Junction (near Cudworth) to Bradford. The first portion from Royston Junction to Dewsbury was constructed, but the rest of the line did not materialize and, in 1919, the powers elapsed. The Midland Railway Company decided not to apply for a renewal and so the project was abandoned.

The Leeds New Line had a relatively short life of only 65 years due in the main to route duplication but some of the station sitings also left something to be desired. The spelling of the station name "Upper Birstal" is the official spelling as this conflicts with present day usage.

Today there are many communities without a railway network where once the everyday life of the town centred on the railway, with many of the towns having two or more stations. The Spen and Birstall valleys are no exception to this although the Calder Valley does still have an operational rail service but this is only a shadow of its former self.

This is called progress. I wonder!

5

**HEATON LODGE AND WORTLEY RAILWAYS.**
Session 1892.
*Sheet N.º 4.*

This is part of the plans provided by the LNWR in conjunction with the 1892 Act. It shows the intended route to be taken through the town and the limit of deviation (indicated by dotted lines).
West Yorkshire Archive Library

HECKMONDWIKE

# Chapter One
## Conception and Planning

In the year 1890 the London & North Western Railway Company (LNWR) was handling ever-increasing traffic along its route across the Pennines between Yorkshire and Lancashire. A considerable amount of freight was being carried from one side of the country to the other: Hull to Liverpool, Newcastle to Manchester with the Yorkshire woollen industry contributing its share, along with the Lancashire cotton industry. There was also coal traffic from large numbers of small mines and ending up in many goods yards and gas works.

The LNWR was finding that it needed extra carrying capacity between Huddersfield and Leeds. The company's existing route at the time ran from Huddersfield through Bradley, Heaton Lodge, Mirfield, Dewsbury, Batley, Morley then on to Leeds and was known as the Leeds, Dewsbury & Manchester Railway. This railway was authorised by the Act of 30th June, 1845 which was vested in the LNWR by the LNWR Act of 9th July, 1847 and opened to the public on 18th September, 1848. The main problem with this route was that a section from Heaton Lodge Junction to Thornhill LNW Junction was actually owned by the Lancashire and Yorkshire Railway Company (L&Y).

By 1894 the LNWR had widened its route across the Pennines to four tracks as far as Heaton Lodge Junction and from there to Thornhill LNW Junction it had to be content with running powers along this L&Y section of the Calder Valley Line. The remainder of the LNWR route to Leeds was only double track which was not easy to enlarge, particularly in three places. Firstly at Dewsbury there was a viaduct on a sharp curve which was flanked by a large textile mill and industrial premises; secondly at Batley the line was carried on a viaduct which ran side by side with a viaduct carrying the Great Northern Railway, and the other problem area of Morley tunnel (nearly two miles long) was by now well known for its problems with mining subsidence.

Having considered this the LNWR looked at alternative routes. There was no easy option, but the Directors of the day decided to build a completely new railway; apart from giving extra route capacity it would also capture new business from the towns it served.

The first scheme to emerge was known as the 1891 plan. This made provision for one double track railway from Heaton Lodge to Wortley via Heckmondwike. The ruling gradient was to be 1 in 70 and three tunnels were included, 580 yds at Heckmondwike, 660 yds at Gomersal and 1808 yds at Gildersome. Estimates which accompanied these plans allowed for expenditure of:

£124,000 on tunnelling,
£38,600 on viaducts, which included the bridge over the River Calder at Battyeford and
£90,000 on stations.
Total expenditure was estimated at £817,913 3s. 6d.

These plans were rejected, the main concern being centred around the junction at Wortley. After modification and re-submission, it came to be known as the 1892 plans.

The 1892 plans made provision for two railways. Railway No. 1 was the main double track route from Heaton Lodge, just stopping short of the junction at Wortley, then continuing as a single track railway to form the up line through the junction. Railway No. 2 was a single track railway forming the down line through the junction at Wortley. This arrangement meant there was to be a "flying junction" at Wortley which would eventually become part of the Farnley Junction complex.

This plan was very similar to the previous 1891 plan in having the same ruling gradient and minimum curves, with these being kept to a radius of 2 furlongs 5 chains. Apart from the alteration to the junction at Wortley, the only other major difference appeared to be the 580 yd tunnel at Heckmondwike, being replaced with a deep cutting.

Estimates which accompanied these revised plans allowed for expenditure of:

£100,720 on tunnelling,
£38,600 on viaducts and
£100,000 on stations
Total expenditure was estimated at £920,270 15s. 7d., this being an increase of more than 10 per cent when set against the 1891 figures, at a time when there was no inflation.

The new 1892 plans were deposited on 28th November, 1891 for inclusion in the 1892 sessions.

The L&Y made a very forceful objection, arguing that there was no need for a second line within the Spen Valley, and offered the use of its own line from Cleckheaton to Mirfield to the LNWR. To have accepted this proposal would have been counter-productive, because the L&Y branch from Spen Valley joined the Calder Valley line at Mirfield, the very area that the LNWR was striving to avoid.

For running powers over the short distance of the L&Y Calder Valley line (from Heaton Lodge Junction to Thornhill LNW Junction) the LNWR had to pay a minimum toll of £4,000 per annum, which increased in proportion to the amount of traffic. During 1892 the LNWR paid £13,000 to the L&Y for this privilege, so with an alternative route there would be no need to exceed the minimum sum, as all traffic which did not require to call at Dewsbury, Batley or Morley, could be re-routed.

The revised plans were approved by Parliament and the Bill given the Royal Assent on 27th June, 1892 as the London and North Western Railway (Heaton Lodge and Wortley Railways) Act (55–56 Vic cap. clxxviii).

The proposed Railway No. 1 was to be 13 miles 2 furlongs 7 chains and 45 links running from Heaton Lodge to Wortley, passing through the townships of Battyeford, Mirfield, Northorpe, Heckmondwike, Liversedge, Cleckheaton, Gomersal and Birstall which meant spanning the three valleys of the Calder, Spen and Birstall. There would be seven passenger stations, all with goods facilities, nearly sixty bridges and viaducts and nearly two miles of tunnelling. The towns of Battyeford and Mirfield being quite close together were to have only one station, and this would be at Battyeford. Maybe it was considered unnecessary to have a station at Mirfield with the L&Y already serving the towns from Huddersfield and Leeds. Another consideration was whether to provide a station at Gildersome, as it would be quite remote from the township itself, with the line being in a deep tunnel at this point. Eventually it was decided to provide a station in the Rooms Lane area of Geldard Road.

A considerable amount of civil engineering work would be required, necessitated by the very hilly terrain; rising from 175 ft above sea level at Heaton Lodge, to the highest point of 465 ft above sea level at Birstall and then rapidly descending to 175 ft above sea level again at Wortley on the outskirts of Leeds.

1892 was in fact quite late in terms of constructing a railway as the majority had been established by then. Towns had started to expand, especially in the industrial north, making route planning difficult and therefore it was another eight years before any trains would run on this particular line.

The railway was planned under the direction of the LNWR's Chief Engineer and most of the work was entrusted to four individuals, these being:

    Mr Frances Stevenson – *Chief Engineer to the LNWR*
    Mr Cooksey – *Mining Engineer*
    Mr Hull – *Chief Negotiator*
    Mr Louis Trench – *Resident Engineer*

During 1892 at one of the Board meetings, Mr L. Trench was appointed as Resident Engineer of the Heaton Lodge and Wortley line from 1st December, 1892 at a salary of £600 per annum, having resigned the position of Chief Engineer to the Great Western Railway. However it was found necessary to engage him earlier from 1st November, 1892 with appropriate adjustments to his salary.

The planning followed a familiar pattern of the LNWR throughout; the bridges were of two basic designs, either stone pillars supporting an iron deck, or a stone bridge with a brick arch, the standard span being 35 or 50 feet depending on the width of the road or railway which required to be spanned. There were a few exceptions where conditions dictated otherwise, such as a few bridges and viaducts built entirely of brick, utilising first quality engineering blue bricks. Another standard feature was the passenger stations, most of which were timber construction, the notable exceptions being Battyeford and Heckmondwike. These had brick platforms paved with stone flags but still retaining the timber building structures.

The signal boxes were all to similar designs, the main difference being that some were all-timber construction, whilst others had the lower half built of brick. Five viaducts were constructed, these were at Mirfield, Heckmondwike, two at Battyeford and a road access viaduct at Cleckheaton. Regarding the tunnels, these were of conventional construction, the longest of which was at Gildersome, the next in length bored at Gomersal with two very short ones at Heckmondwike. There were also two short single-bore tunnels at Heaton Lodge, to allow the line to pass beneath the L&Y Calder Valley route.

55 & 56 Vict.]   *London and North Western*   [**Ch. clxxviii.**]
*Railway (Heaton Lodge and Wortley Railways) Act,* 1892.

### CHAPTER clxxviii.

An Act for empowering the London and North Western  A.D. 1892.
Railway Company to construct new Railways in the
West Riding of the county of York to be called the
Heaton Lodge and Wortley Railways and for other
purposes.                           [27th June 1892.]

**W**HEREAS it is expedient that the London and North Western
Railway Company (in this Act called "the Company")
should be empowered to make the new railways in the West Riding
of the county of York in this Act mentioned :

And whereas plans and sections showing the respective lines and
levels of the railways by this Act authorised to be constructed and
also books of reference containing the names of the owners and
lessees or reputed owners and lessees and of the occupiers of the
lands required or which may be taken for the purposes or under the
powers of this Act were duly deposited with the clerk of the peace
for the West Riding of the county of York which plans sections and
books of reference are in this Act respectively referred to as the
deposited plans sections and books of reference :

And whereas it is expedient that the Company should be
empowered to raise additional capital for the purposes of this Act
and for the general purposes of their undertaking and to apply their
funds to the purposes of this Act :

And whereas the purposes of this Act cannot be effected without
the authority of Parliament :

May it therefore please Your Majesty that it may be enacted and
be it enacted by the Queen's most Excellent Majesty by and with
the advice and consent of the Lords Spiritual and Temporal and
Commons in this present Parliament assembled and by the authority
of the same as follows (that is to say) :—

[*Price* 2s.]

The front page of the 1892 Act for the Heaton Lodge and Wortley Railways.

[55 & 56 VICT.]   *London and North Western*   [**Ch. clxxviii.**]
   *Railway (Heaton Lodge and Wortley Railways) Act,* 1892.

to the levels shown on the deposited sections the following railways  ·A.D. 1892.
with all proper stations sidings roads approaches works and
conveniences connected therewith respectively and may enter upon
take and use such of the lands delineated on the deposited plans
and described in the deposited books of reference as may be required
for the purposes thereof or in connection therewith:

The railways hereinbefore referred to and authorised by this Act
are—

> Two railways (to be called the Heaton Lodge and Wortley
> Railways) to be wholly situate in the West Riding of the
> county of York :
>> (1) Railway No. 1 thirteen miles two furlongs seven chains
>> and forty-five links in length commencing in the township
>> and parish of Kirkheaton by a junction with the
>> Company's Huddersfield and Manchester Railway and
>> terminating in the township of Wortley in the parish
>> of Leeds by a junction with the Company's Leeds
>> and Dewsbury Railway :
>> (2) Railway No. 2 six furlongs five chains and sixty-five
>> links in length commencing in the township of Beeston
>> in the parish of Leeds by a junction with Railway No. 1
>> and terminating in the township of Wortley in the parish
>> of Leeds by a junction with the said Leeds and Dewsbury
>> Railway.

5. The railways shall for all purposes whatever be part of the  Tolls &c. for
Company's undertaking and for the use thereof and for the  new railways
conveyance of passengers and parcels by passenger train thereon the  &c.
Company may demand and take the tolls rates and charges authorised
by the Act (local and personal) ninth and tenth Victoria chapter
two hundred and four entitled " An Act to Consolidate the London
" and Birmingham Grand Junction and Manchester and Birmingham
" Railway Companies " and for the conveyance of merchandise
thereon the Company may demand and take the maximum rates
and charges authorised by the London and North Western Railway
Company (Rates and Charges) Order Confirmation Act 1891 in
respect of the railways not therein specially mentioned.

6. The Company may divert alter and stop up in the manner  Power to
shown upon the deposited plans and sections any roads delineated  divert roads
on the said plans and described in the deposited books of reference  deposited
and when and as in each case the new portion of any road is made  plans.
to the satisfaction of two justices and is open for public use may
stop up and cause to be discontinued as a road so much of the

The relevant page of the 1892 Act covering the Railways.

## THE LEEDS NEW LINE

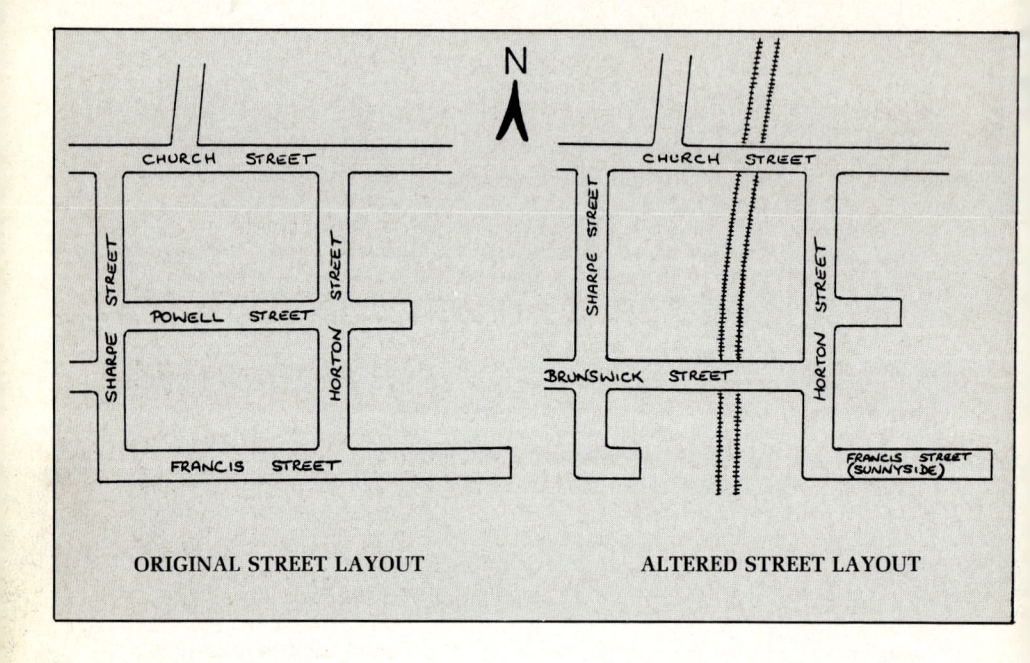

**ORIGINAL STREET LAYOUT**

**ALTERED STREET LAYOUT**

Planning of the line and authorisations took more than five years, because of the large number of individual land and property owners, together with local problems, especially at Heckmondwike where the proposed route cut through a heavily populated area of the old town. This required acquisition of large amounts of property and the re-housing of the occupants. It is interesting to note the company had an obligation to provide new housing within one mile of that which was being demolished.

A small community existed in Walkley Bottoms, and the tenants, along with the Heckmondwike Board of Health, tried unsuccessfully to get the LNWR to provide a vehicle underpass at the occupation level crossing on the L&Y Ravensthorpe branch. Some of these houses had to be demolished to make way for the new railway, but the new replacement houses were said to be far superior, both in design and facilities.

During the months preceding the passing of the 1892 Bill the company negotiated with its major opponents with great success, so that the only major opposition remaining was from the L&Y Railway company. Relations between the two companies at this time must have been very strained, because the LNWR decided to employ its own staff on the L&Y Cleckheaton branch. This also involved the provision of 20 horses and 26 drays, plus an office at Heckmondwike.

When the 1892 Bill received the Royal Assent, the Engineer was instructed to proceed with the land plans so that the company negotiator, Mr

## CONCEPTION AND PLANNING 13

Hull, could finalise his dealings with the many smaller landowners.

In June 1894 there was a major conflict over the proposed site of Heckmondwike passenger station. The following extract is taken from the *Heckmondwike Herald and Courier* dated 14th June, 1894.

> The Local Board of Health opposed a Bill to close two footpaths which run between High Street and Cemetery Road, on the grounds that the railway company proposed to replace them with a footbridge over the line.
>
> The Local Board claimed to have a 12 yards wide road constructed to run parallel with the new station so that they would agree to the footpaths being closed.
>
> Mr James Saville, surveyor to the Local Board, estimated that the new road would be 200 yards in length and would cost £1,010 for works, £800 for land and £400 for a retaining wall, altogether about £2,200.
>
> Mr Frances Stevenson, the company engineer, was then called and put the cost of road construction and land at £5,480. The works would cost £1,900 and the land and buildings £2,500.
>
> The company said they were prepared to hand over £2,000 in land and money towards the improvement. After further discussions it was decided that the Local Board should make the road, and the company hand over to them £700. A settlement was accordingly agreed.

The outcome of this agreement is today's Bath Road which runs parallel with the station site between the High Street and Cemetery Road.

In 1895 a scheme was put forward to block-up the bottom 55 yds of Francis Street and the bottom 55 yds of Powell Street at Heckmondwike (both being between Sharpe Street and Horton Street), and to construct a new road 55 yds long (see *plan*) being a continuation of Brunswick Street.

As can be seen, this made it necessary to build one road overbridge, rather than two. The bottom part of Francis Street that remains today is now called Sunnyside. The name probably came about because all the houses face towards the south, and also avoids confusion with the top part of Francis Street, this being provided for by the LNWR as part of the Eighty Houses development, and (sited to the east of the accompanying map) at the other side of some playing fields.

Additional powers were obtained by the London and North Western Railway Act (58–59 Vic. cap. cxxvi) which received the Royal Assent on 6th July, 1895.

This Act allowed the company to substitute the 261 yds-long viaduct at Heckmondwike for a solid embankment of "170 yds or thereabouts". It also permitted the company to acquire additional land at Heckmondwike adjoining the L&Y Railway Ravensthorpe branch, plus the stopping-up and re-routing of various footpaths along the line. Also included in these powers was the stopping-up of Rooms Lane bridle road at Gildersome, for a distance of "410 yds or thereabouts", this being from the Geldard Road, the new road construction to be carried over the railway by means of a bridge.

It is also known that some larger houses were dismantled and moved to an alternative location. Finding which houses were involved has not been an easy task, but two of them have been located. A house which now stands at the corner of Horton Street and Sunnyside in Heckmondwike was moved from Church Street in 1897. At Liversedge a house named "The Royds", which stood at the top of Royds Park, was, in 1898, transferred to its present site in Whitechapel Road, Cleckheaton. Ironically in 1965, this same house again became threatened when the M62 motorway was being planned, but in the event only lost part of its garden.

A protection clause was obtained in 1898 with respect to the Midland Railway proposed line which was to run by the side of and over the Heaton Lodge and Wortley line at Liversedge. This provided protection so that LNWR company property at Cleckheaton and Heckmondwike could not be interfered with.

To include all the land dealings involved in the construction of this line would require a very lengthy chapter indeed, and therefore hopefully sufficient have been detailed to give a glimpse of the very complex nature of the work involved. Sadly Mr Hull passed away in August 1898, and one wonders if it was the enormous workload which led to his death.

The Seal of the London & North Western Railway.

## Chapter Two
## Construction of the Line

As already stated, before the Heaton Lodge and Wortley Railway could be constructed, large numbers of people needed to be rehoused especially in the Heckmondwike area and property demolished in order to make a route through the town, this also applied to a lesser degree at Battyeford and Birstall.

In December 1893 the LNWR submitted to the Local Board of Health (which was the forerunner to the Urban District Council) proposals to acquire 126 houses in various parts of Heckmondwike. Over 60 per cent of these houses were occupied by what the LNWR called "the labouring class".

Plans for the new houses were approved in April 1894 providing for the construction of a total of 80 houses on land owned by Sir Francis Sharpe Powell, Bart, MP, situated at the top of Church Street. The railway company put this work out to tender in July 1894, which was awarded in the same month to Messrs Robinson & Crowther to build all 80 houses in six blocks for a total sum of £20,267 10s. 0d. At the same time, a contract for making up streets was awarded to Messrs Smith & Boocock for £1,786. It is of little surprise that the new streets were named Powell Street and Francis Street and, locally, this complex is known as the "Eighty Houses".

Legal power was sought in October 1894 to dispense with the erection of any labouring class housing at Birstall, but at Battyeford it was necessary to construct 12 houses and once again in August 1895 the contract was awarded to Messrs Robinson & Crowther for £3,048, at the same price per house as the 80 they were building at Heckmondwike. In addition, the railway company's cost towards street-making was £300.

Referring back to the actual railway construction contract, it was divided into six individual contracts; three for the civil engineering work and three for the stations with the LNWR looking after the railway installations and ballasting of track.

> Contract No. 1, *Mirfield Section.*
> Civil engineering work from Heaton Lodge to a point on the Northorpe side of Park Colliery.
>
> Contract No. 2, *Wortley Section.*
> Civil engineering work from and including Gomersal tunnel to Wortley.
>
> Contract No. 3, *Spen Valley Section.*
> Civil engineering work from Park Colliery up to but not including Gomersal tunnel.
>
> Contract No. 4.
> Passenger and Goods stations at Battyeford and Northorpe.
>
> Contract No. 5.
> Passenger and Goods stations at Heckmondwike, Liversedge and Cleckheaton.
>
> Contract No. 6.
> Passenger and Goods stations at Gomersal, Upper Birstal and Gildersome.

The Resident Engineer, Mr Trench, had a deputy appointed by the name of Mr McGregor who was given special responsibility for the Spen Valley

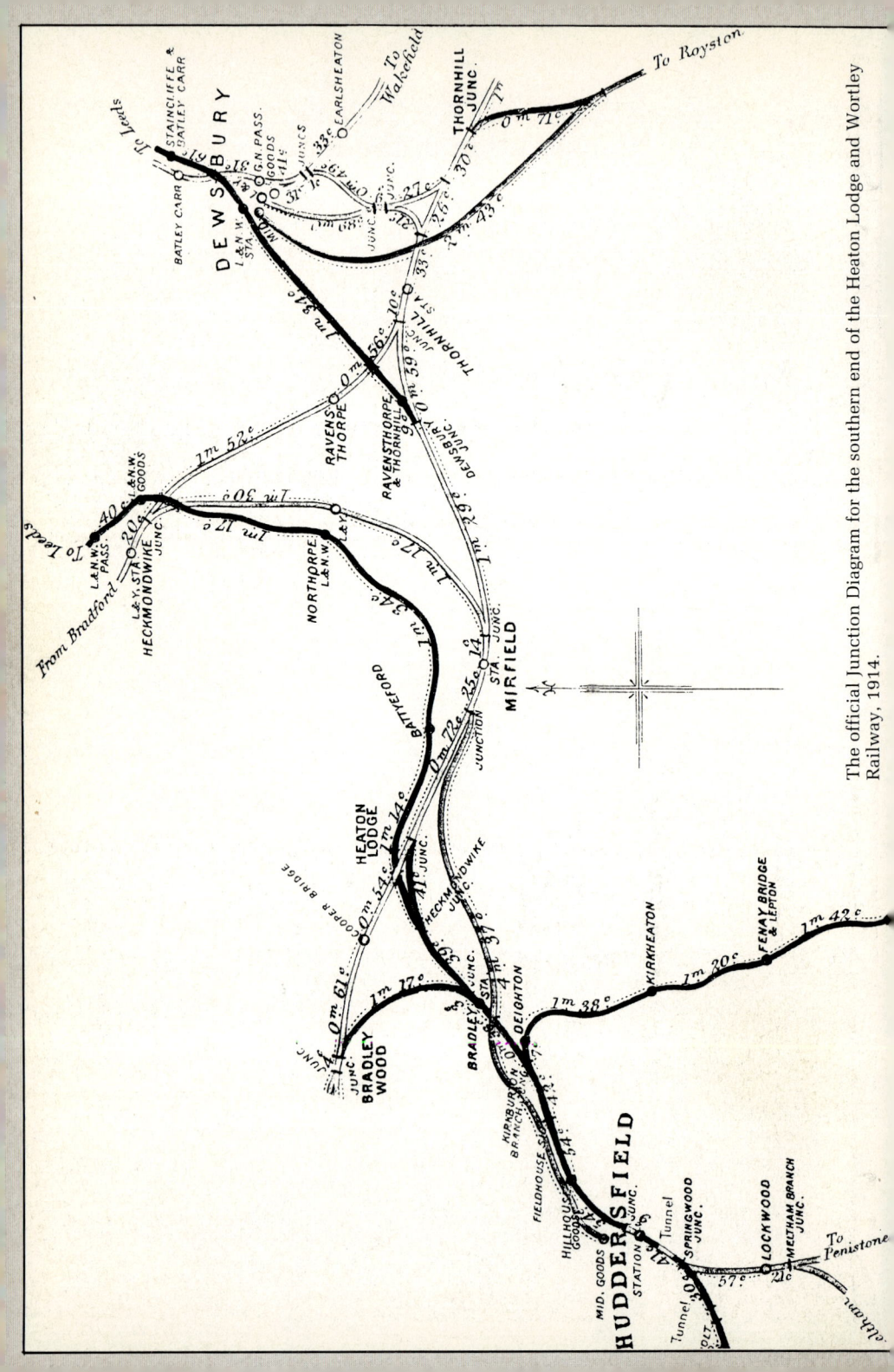

The official Junction Diagram for the southern end of the Heaton Lodge and Wortley Railway, 1914.

Spen Valley Junction seen here in October 1962 showing stored coaching stock in the sidings at Heaton Lodge. The Heaton Lodge & Wortley line branches off to the left.
*Peter E. Baughan*

Passing Heaton Lodge South Junction, No. 47 518 heads a Newcastle to Liverpool Lime Street service on 15th February, 1985.
*Author*

The rather unusual tunnel/bridge carrying the curved line beneath the Lancashire and Yorkshire Railway at Heaton Lodge.  *Author*

This footbridge crosses the line at Heaton Lodge near where the ex-L&Y signal box once stood. There was a very similar footbridge which crossed the line at the top of New Street, about halfway between the stations at Cleckheaton and Liversedge.  *Author*

Section. This allowed Mr Trench to devote more time to the more difficult Wortley Section.

It appears that contracts were let in numerical order. No. 1 was awarded on 24th April, 1895 to Messrs Graham & Sons of Huddersfield for £71,645 15s. 6d., but for some unknown reason this tender (which was the lowest received) must have proved unsatisfactory, because the contract was re-awarded on 15th May, 1895 to Messrs J. Wilson & Sons of Huddersfield who had tendered £75,340 16s. 0d.

A remarkable total of fourteen tenders were received for Contract No. 2 which the LNWR Chief Engineer estimated to be worth £287,500. This consisted of 6¾ miles of trackwork and included two tunnels. Once again the lowest tender was accepted and awarded on 18th December, 1895 to Messrs Baldry & Yerburgh for £255,485 19s. 9d.

Contract No. 3 was not let until 14th October, 1896; twelve tenders were received for this four mile stretch through the Spen Valley which the company Engineer estimated to be worth £108,000. The lowest tender was accepted from Messrs Monk & Newell of Bootle for £100,833 11s. 6d.

Contracts Nos. 4, 5 & 6 (for the construction of the stations) were not let to tender, but were offered to and accepted by the contractors already engaged on the first three contracts, for station construction in their respective areas.

Contract 4 was estimated to be worth £15,000, Contract 5 was estimated to be worth £25,000 and Contract 6 was estimated to be worth £17,000.

It is interesting to note that these estimates are greatly reduced from the estimates produced with the 1892 plan which allowed £100,000 for all the stations, both passenger and goods.

Another major contract connected with the line concerned the purchase of slag ballast. As large quantities would be required for the Heaton Lodge & Wortley Railway, Crewe enlargement and other minor work, the LNWR entered into a contract with their supplier Mr J. Freakley to supply 200,000 tons per annum (from October 1898) for a period of three years at a cost of 2s. 0d. per ton. The company installed a siding so that this ballast could be supplied from a slag heap at Golds Green which was situated on the South Staffordshire Line, ½ mile on the Walsall side of Great Bridge station.

Once construction was under way the company received two letters from the clergy. The Rev. H.W. How of Mirfield and the Rev. R.M. Howard of Gomersal asked the company to subscribe towards the support of a Navvy Mission for the men employed on the works at Mirfield and Gomersal. Both these requests were declined and the clergymen advised to approach the contractors who had been engaged to carry out the work.

Contract No. 1, the Mirfield section, was the simplest to construct with no unforeseen problems arising and therefore the works were completed in good time (by 17th May, 1899) and the stations finished by 19th July, 1899.

The LNWR now had in effect a short 2¾ miles branch containing two stations, so they decided to open it on 18th September, 1899 for freight traffic only serving Battyeford & Mirfield and Northorpe.

Col. Addison inspected the new Heckmondwike Junction at Heaton Lodge on 27th September, 1899 and the Board of Trade approval was received.

## THE LEEDS NEW LINE

Taken from a point where the present Heaton Lodge North Junction is now situated, this view shows how the line climbed away to the left over Battyeford girder bridge and the viaducts beyond.
*Peter E. Baughan*

Heaton Lodge North Jn was built in 1970 to simplify conflicting traffic routes using part of the redundant Heaton Lodge and Wortley Railway. Steam hauled specials occasionally make an appearance, one such working was "The West Riding" charter hauled by No. 777 *Sir Lamiel* on 18th May, 1985. The old trackbed to Battyeford can be seen to climb away in front of the locomotive.
*Author*

## CONSTRUCTION OF THE LINE 21

The remains of Battyeford viaduct in 1984. Part of the structure has been dismantled at the far end where the passenger station was located. *Author*

Battyeford station looking towards the goods yard. The station staff are standing on the platform used by trains to Leeds. *Roy Brook*

Heckmondwike viaduct crossing the River Spen.  *Author's Collection*

Except for the signal box name and the "Trans-Pennine" dmu about to cross Heckmondwike viaduct, this scene, photographed on 1st October, 1962, has changed very little since 1900, although I don't think the LNWR would have tolerated such untidiness. It also provides a splendid opportunity to view the man-made plateau which stretches away from the left side of the train.  *Peter E. Baughan*

Contract No. 2, the Wortley section, had the heaviest constructional workload and should have been completed by 30th June, 1898 which was the 2½ year timespan allowed. The contractors met with exceptional difficulties in the area of Gildersome tunnel because of the old coal workings. Two cuttings, one of which was at Birstall, turned out to be hard rock instead of the soft surface material which had been reckoned on. Unless alternative means of excavation could be adopted, these cuttings were estimated to take another two years to complete, so the contractors proposed the use of a number of steam cranes working at several places simultaneously to expedite the work. They also said that this extra work would cost an additional £6,442. The LNWR pointed out that if agreed to, it would be stipulated that this extra allowance would be made only on condition that the whole of the remaining works were completed by 30th September, 1899. If the cuttings were not finished at that date, no allowance whatever would be forthcoming for any quantity of rock excavated beyond the contract price of 1s. 2d. per cubic yard.

To complicate matters further, Mr Joseph Haigh of Victoria Colliery, Bruntcliffe gave notice to the company in February 1898 that he intended to work the black lead, coal and iron-stone under the newly excavated tunnel at Gildersome. The LNWR became very concerned about this especially with the mines lying at a depth of about 600 ft. It was decided to serve a compulsory purchase order on that portion of the mine (about 7½ acres) that was directly involved.

Mr Haigh claimed the value of the mine to be £4,682 but Mr Cooksey (the LNWR mining engineer) valued it at £3,000 so the case was submitted for arbitration. At the hearing, Mr H.S. Childs (mining engineer of Wakefield) awarded £3,806 1s. 6d. to Mr Haigh as a "fair value". To protect their interests in case of further claims, the LNWR decided to purchase from Miss Booth mines which were under Geldard Road and the station area at Birstall for the sum of £218 15s. 0d.

Contract No. 3, the Spen Valley section (although only about four miles in length) was a very heavily engineered section. The original plans for a viaduct 261 yds long were amended in the 1895 Bill providing a shorter viaduct together with an earth embankment. Coal mines under the proposed viaduct were purchased for £600 so that firm foundations could be established, and, after their previous experience at Gildersome, the LNWR decided in August 1899 to purchase a further mine under the station area at Heckmondwike for £260 10s. 0d., belonging to the late Mr E. Brooke. The depth of this mine varied from 180 ft to 720 ft and if left to be worked could have given rise to subsidence of the station buildings, track and Cemetery Road bridge.

In October 1896 Heckmondwike U.D.C. requested that the company construct a wider road bridge, 30 ft instead of the proposed 20 ft to carry Jeremy Lane, at an estimated extra cost of £120. The council were willing to contribute £75 towards the total and also to pave the enlarged area. The company accepted this proposal provided the council agreed to divert the proposed roads called Lower North Road and Hill House Road so that they did not cross the railway. Under an agreement (dated 2nd June, 1892)

The original Heckmondwike Junction on the ex-L&Y line. In the distance the diesel-hauled express is on the Heaton Lodge & Wortley line with the locomotive on bridge No. 21 over the Ravensthorpe branch and the rear of the train on the viaduct.

*Peter E. Baughan*

A closer view from a train as it passes over bridge No. 21. The occupation level crossing leading to Walkley Bottoms can be seen at the left of this view, with the footpath subway this side of the gates.

*G.B. Goldthorp*

# CONSTRUCTION OF THE LINE 25

between the West Riding Union Banking Company as trustees of the late James Firth, Thomas Freeman Firth and the Heckmondwike Local Board, these roads were proposed to cross the railway. This technicality was thrown into the lap of Mr Hull to disentangle and, once resolved, a wider bridge was built.

Heckmondwike U.D.C., in July 1899, made two more requests, firstly that the company agree to discharge their interest in what was later to be called Bath Road, of which they were part-owners. This was eventually agreed to and £30 was accepted from the council. Also at this time the council was considering building a swimming baths on an adjacent site to the station.

The other request was that a footpath be constructed on company property between Victoria Street and Cemetery Road and an agreement was reached provided the council paid a fee of £1 per annum. The company were also to be allowed to "stop" the footpath annually to preserve its rights.

*(Above)* Part of the eighty houses complex at Heckmondwike, built for the LNWR by Robinson & Crowther in 1894/95 to replace older property being cleared to make way for the new railway and, *(below)*, the twelve houses at Battyeford are built to exactly the same design, as described on page 15. *(Both) Author*

(*Above*) That part of the railway at Heckmondwike in the 48 ft deep cutting to the north of Walkley Lane bridge. The house to the left of the church steeple was moved from Church Street by the LNWR in 1898. (*Below*) The same view in June 1985 with a train of fuel oil heading for Liversedge.   *Top: Peter E. Baughan and bottom: Author*

# Chapter Three
## The Route Described

The new railway commenced at Heaton Lodge, branching away from the existing Huddersfield to Leeds (via Dewsbury) line, some 500 yds or so to the south-west of Heaton Lodge Junction, at a new junction to be named Heckmondwike Junction. The line immediately descended to a level under the four-tracks-wide Calder Valley line of the L&Y Railway. Here the line was on a curve so that this bridge was constructed in the form of two single bore tunnels. Where the line climbed past the back of the L&Y Heaton Lodge Junction signal box, an iron footbridge was provided to overcarry a path.

Further on at a gradient of 1 in 90, the line crossed the River Calder on a single span, latticed, Warren riveted bridge of 267 feet, weighing 700 tons. The excessive gradient was called for to provide a minimum headroom of 15 ft above the river's average water level.

To span the valley and reach Battyeford station, the line was carried upon two viaducts, a short span of 89 yds built in stone and a longer section of 193 yds built of blue engineering brick usually referred to as Battyeford Viaduct. The only unusual thing about the passenger station at Battyeford was the fact that about half the length of each platform was constructed over the road bridge and viaduct. Battyeford station had a substantial goods yard which included a large stone warehouse, a loading dock, stables and the coal merchants' yard.

Battyeford coal yard had an interesting history of its own, being fully utilized throughout the life of the railway. To my knowledge three coal merchants worked from the yard, namely Mann & Hardy, Mathew Hesp & Son and Percy Hargreaves. The largest of these was Mann & Hardy Ltd, known in the early years as J.T. Mann (later J.T. Mann & Hardy) and finally as Mann & Hardy Ltd.

Mathew Hesp & Son started working from the yard in the early part of the century; this company is still a family concern and working under the same name.

Battyeford in the early days had quite a sizeable stock of cart-horses, with J.T. Mann & Hardy owning six, Mathew Hesp & Son owning one, and Percy Hargreaves owning one. The LNWR also owned a few for delivering goods from the warehouse, which seems to have been mainly grain for Sutcliffe Maltsters in Station Road, Mirfield. In about 1950, horses and carts gave way to motorised transport and in later years the tipping dock was mainly used by a company named Hubert Maughan, for the loading of scrap metal on to wagons for transportation by rail.

Leaving Battyeford goods yard the line was carried on another large viaduct of 190 yds, built of blue engineering brick and known as Mirfield viaduct. Passing through a cutting to reach Northorpe, the railway was crossed by various roads, one of which, (Pinfold Lane) had to be raised by five feet to obtain the necessary clearance. Although Northorpe had a conventional timber station, the goods yard was very small with only two sidings and it was the only yard not to be provided with a warehouse.

After Northorpe station it was only a short distance to Park Colliery, which was situated midway between Northorpe and Heckmondwike goods

# HEATON LODGE

X = SIGNAL POST.

AREA OF SEWAGE WORKS

TO LEEDS
FOOTBRIDGE
SIGNAL BOX
SIDINGS
L & Y. CALDER VALLEY LINE
HEATON LODGE JUNCTION
HUDDERSFIELD & LEEDS JNT
SIGNAL BOX
HEATON LODGE & WORTLEY LINE
SIDINGS
L.N.W.R.

HECKMONDWIKE JUNCTION 1899 – 1923
SPEN VALLEY JUNCTION 1923 – 1970
HEATON LODGE SOUTH JUNCTION 1970

SIGNAL BOX
RIVER CALDER
RIVER COLNE
TO HUDDERSFIELD
CANAL
LOCK

## APRIL 1970 to APRIL 1988

OLD TRACKBED TO BATTYEFORD
FOOTBRIDGE
HEATON LODGE NORTH JUNCTION
HEATON LODGE SOUTH JUNCTION

Redrawn from the 1907 Ordnance Survey Map.

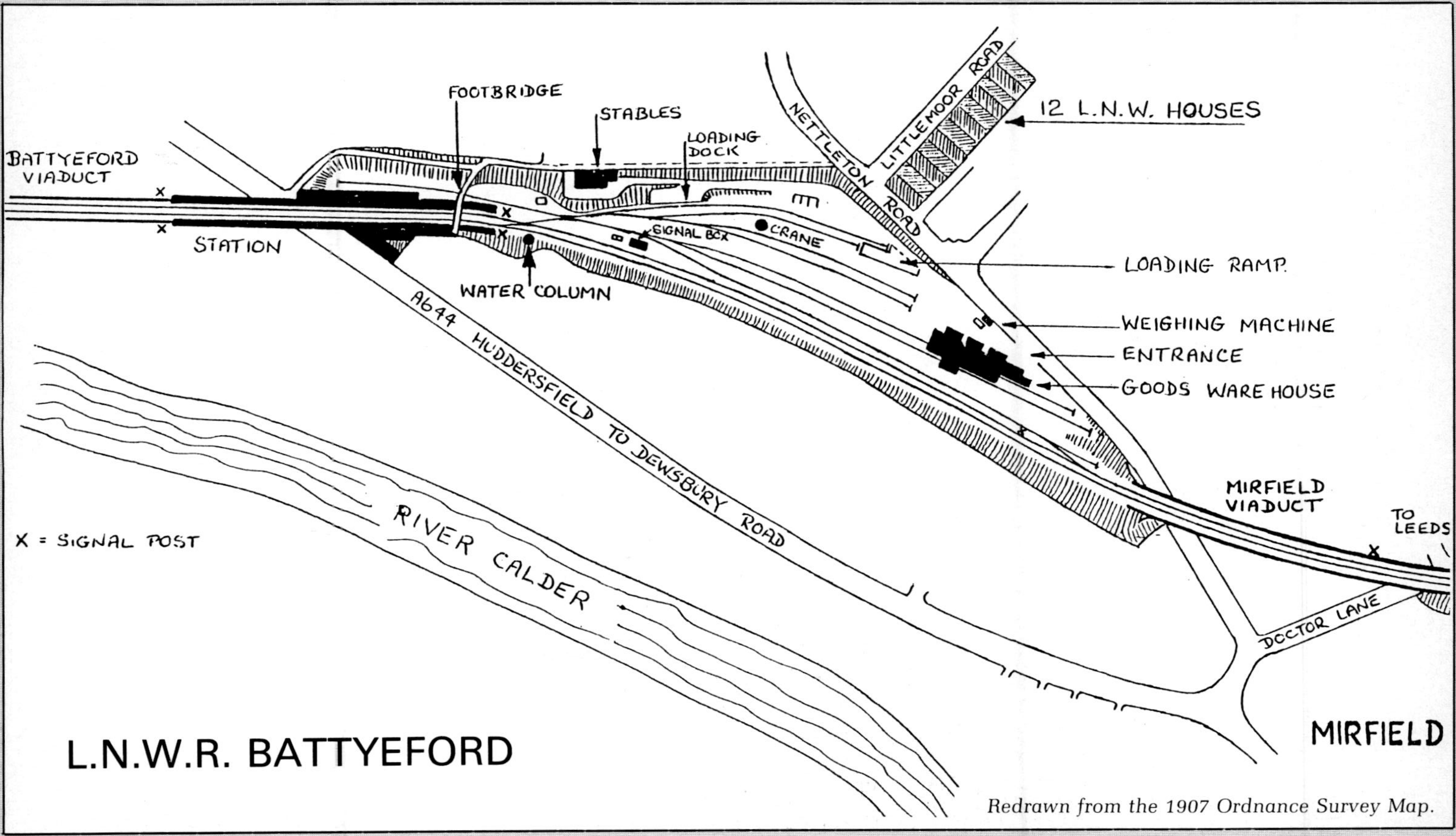
FOOTBRIDGE
STABLES
LOADING DOCK
12 L.N.W. HOUSES
BATTYEFORD VIADUCT
NETTLETON ROAD
LITTLEMOOR ROAD
STATION
SIGNAL BOX
CRANE
LOADING RAMP.
WATER COLUMN
WEIGHING MACHINE
ENTRANCE
GOODS WARE HOUSE
A644 HUDDERSFIELD TO DEWSBURY ROAD
MIRFIELD VIADUCT
TO LEEDS
X = SIGNAL POST
RIVER CALDER
DOCTOR LANE
MIRFIELD
L.N.W.R. BATTYEFORD
Redrawn from the 1907 Ordnance Survey Map.

# L.N.W.R. NORTHORPE

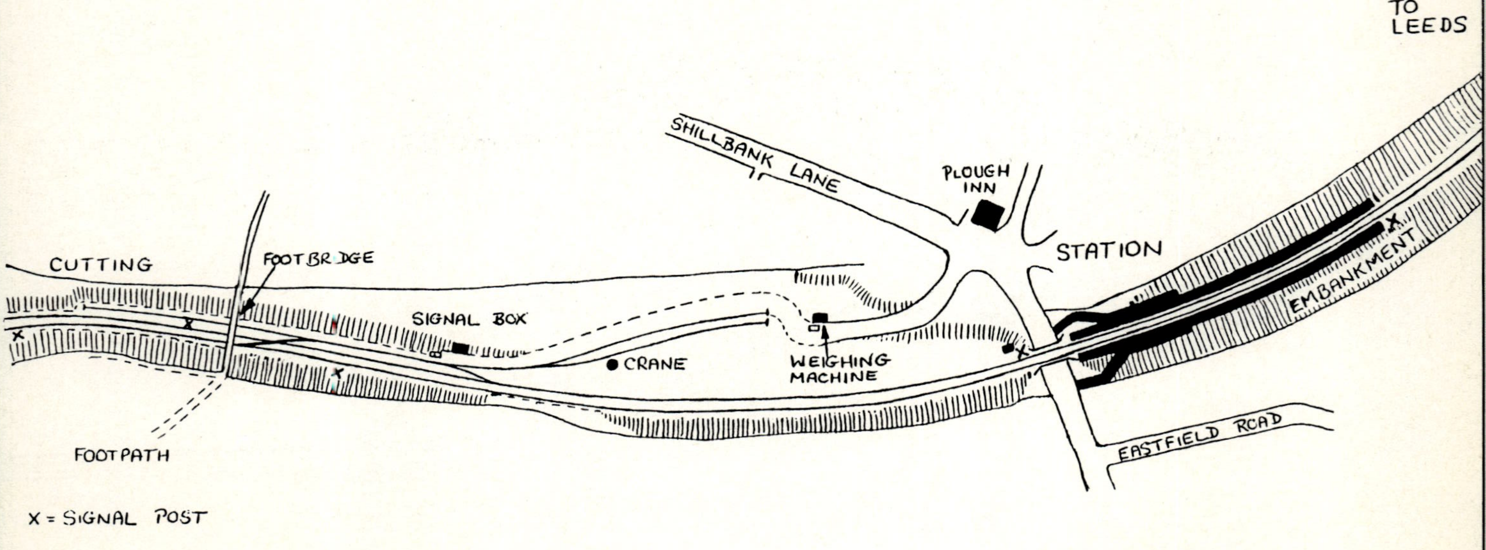


*Redrawn from the 1907 Ordnance Survey Map.*

# L.M.S. NORTHORPE HIGHER

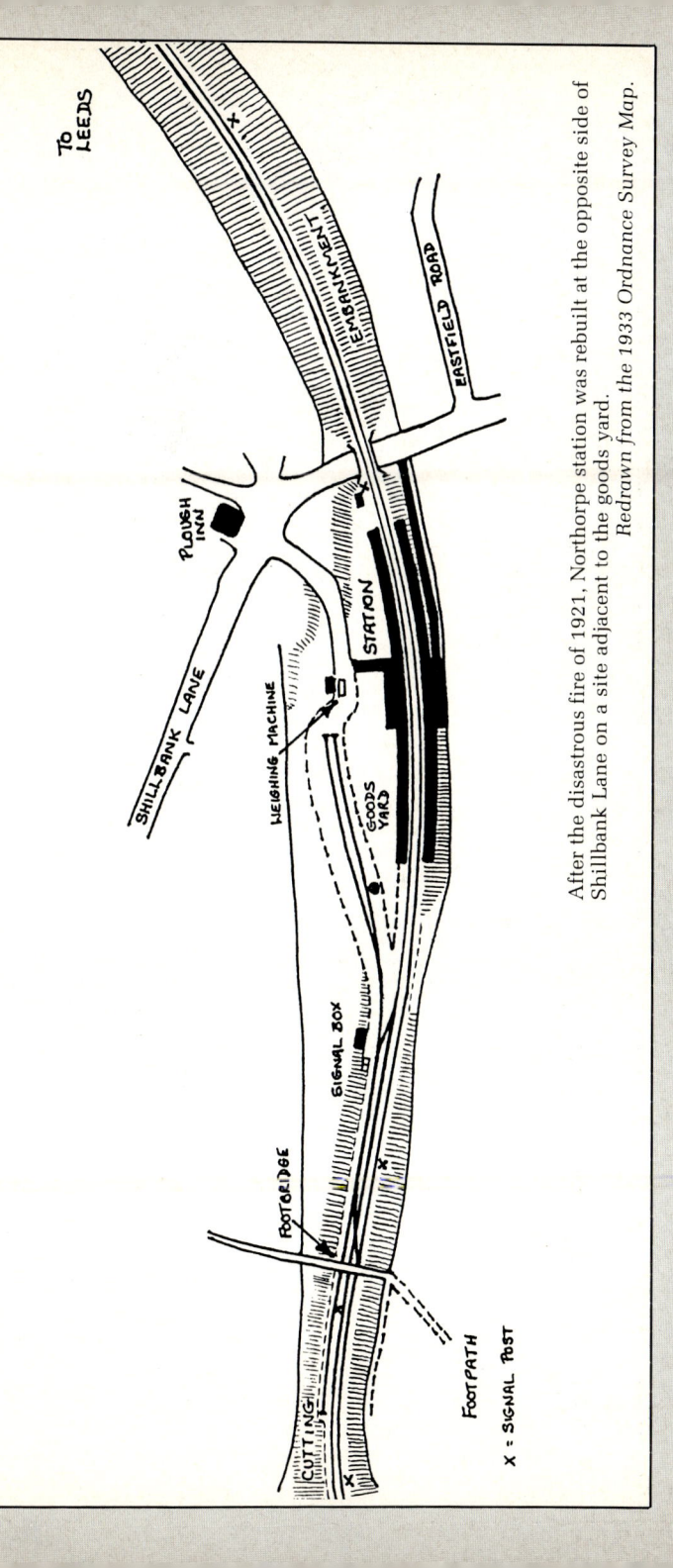

TO LEEDS

EASTFIELD ROAD

EMBANKMENT

PLOUGH INN

SHILLBANK LANE

WEIGHING MACHINE

STATION

GOODS YARD

SIGNAL BOX

FOOTBRIDGE

CUTTING

FOOTPATH

X = SIGNAL POST

After the disastrous fire of 1921, Northorpe station was rebuilt at the opposite side of Shillbank Lane on a site adjacent to the goods yard.
Redrawn from the 1933 Ordnance Survey Map.

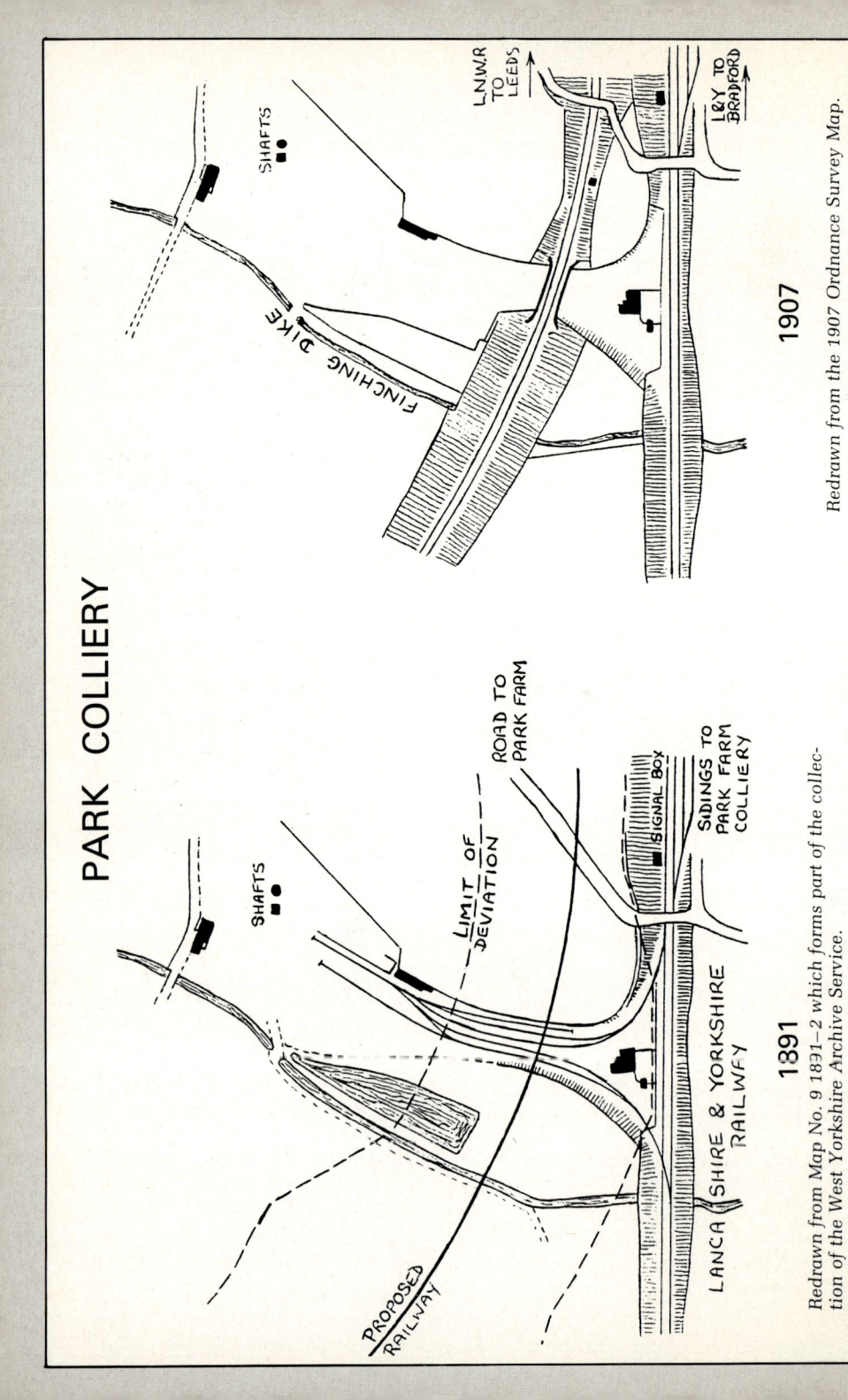

# PARK COLLIERY

**1891**

Redrawn from Map No. 9 1891–2 which forms part of the collection of the West Yorkshire Archive Service.

**1907**

Redrawn from the 1907 Ordnance Survey Map.

yard. It was served by the L&Y Railway (which was opened in 1848) with a branch from Low Moor down the Spen Valley and then on to Mirfield (via Northorpe). The L&Y did not provide a station at Northorpe until 1891 which was probably inspired by the LNWR considering an alternative route and intending also to provide a station at Northorpe.

The LNWR planned and built the new line at a higher level than the L&Y Railway, so it was necessary to span the coal sidings at Park Colliery. This was achieved with a three-arch bridge, each arch having a 25 ft span and being 14 ft 6 in. high. By 1907 the colliery had closed down and the sidings dismantled so this three-arch bridge had quickly been made redundant. At some later time this bridge was demolished and the gap infilled to make a continuous earth embankment.

I visited this area a few times in the mid-1950s on wanderings during my school summer holidays but I have no recollection of seeing the bridge. On a more recent visit, however, in 1984, close examination revealed some stone walling (mixed with the earth embankment) which could well be the remains of a bridge.

The only other alteration in this area was to the road leading to Park Farm, a slight deviation was made so that it would cross the new line at a right angle making for a simpler construction.

Leaving Park Colliery the line passed over the L&Y Mirfield branch at Heckmondwike, on a bridge very similar to the one used to cross the River Calder at Battyeford, but this being only 150 ft long.

From here the line had to cross from one side of the Spen Valley to the other and the original plan of 1891 was to build a viaduct 261 yds long, similar to the one at Battyeford. Most of the line through Heckmondwike being in a deep cutting, the LNWR obtained power in the 1895 Act to alter this to a shorter viaduct plus an earth embankment. This arrangement provided for a site locally to tip the excavations and probably reduce the cost of Contract No. 3. The outcome was a steel or iron viaduct 80 yds long supported on brick pillars, plus an earth embankment which formed a very large man-made plateau.

Heckmondwike was the only place where the goods yard and passenger station were not adjacent, this was due to the geographical nature of the area. The deep cutting was spanned by nine bridges and two tunnels, 50 yds long; the bridges were all to the same design in stone with a brick-lined arch except the ones at Cook Lane and Walkley Lane. These were iron girders with jack arches supported on stone pillars.

Where the railway surfaced from the deep cutting at Cook Lane, stands Heckmondwike Old Hall. This house dates back to at least the 17th century and is important not only for its age but because Joseph Priestley lived here as a boy. Joseph Priestley was born at Birstall in 1733 but spent most of his childhood at Heckmondwike, living with his Aunt Sarah Keighley at the Old Hall. Priestley, during his early years at Heckmondwike, is best remembered for his discovery of oxygen, which came about by observing the behaviour of spiders in sealed glass jars. Later in life he emigrated to America where he lived until his death in 1804.

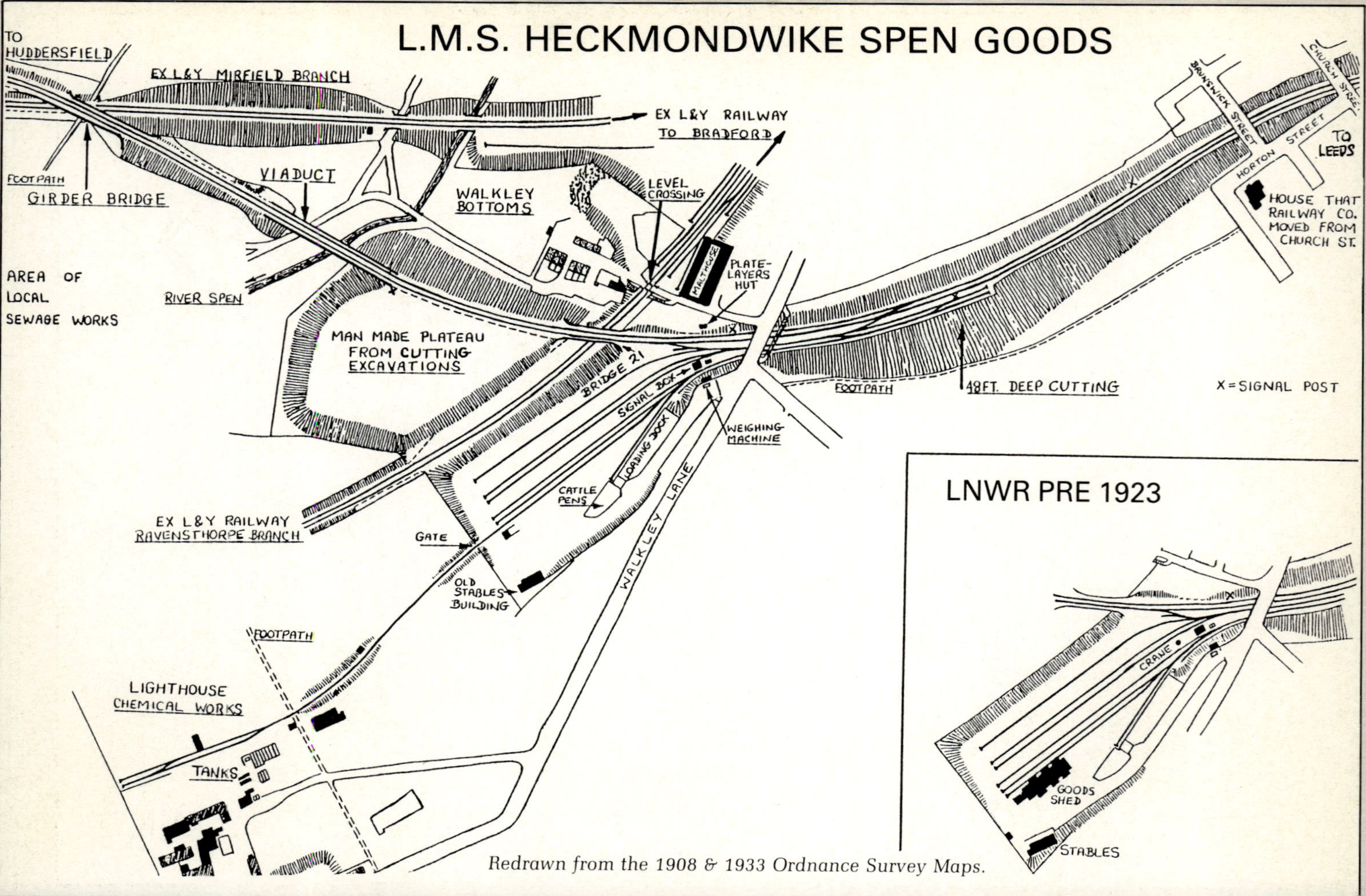


Redrawn from the 1908 & 1933 Ordnance Survey Maps.

# L.N.W.R. HECKMONDWIKE STATION

TO LEEDS

OLD HALL
NEW NORTH ROAD
50 YARD TUNNEL
BRIDGE ST.
JEREMY LANE
PARK ROAD
KING ST.
VICTORIA STREET
FOOTPATH
LYNN SQUARE ST.
CEMETERY ROAD
PLATE LAYERS HUT
SIGNAL BOX
VEHICLE ENTRANCE
BATH STREET
HIGH STREET
MARKET PLACE
TOWN CENTRE
SPARROW PARK
50 YARD TUNNEL
STATION ENTRANCE
JAMES STREET
CHURCH STREET
BRUNSWICK ST.
SQUARE ST.
HORTON ST.
FOOTPATH

X = SIGNAL POST

The area covered by this map to the point at Cook Lane is very built up and heavily populated.

Redrawn from the 1908 Ordnance Survey Map.

The Old Hall and its outbuildings came totally within the limit of deviation for the railway. In 1891 the description of the property was, house, garden, greenhouse, barn, mistels, stables, coach-house, yards, sheds, occupation road and outbuildings. Most of this property was swept away for construction of the line, but the owners of the property and the railway company must have come to some agreement over the Hall because only part of one wing was demolished. Maybe if the owners at the time (listed as Thomas Freeman Firth, Josiah Firth and Edwin Firth) had been more forceful it might have been unnecessary to demolish any part of the Old Hall, had some sort of retaining wall been built. The building has now been restored to nearly its former self and is in use today as a Public House.

At the other side of the line, opposite the Old Hall, was a coal mine known as Victoria Colliery. In June 1898 the railway company leased a section of land to the colliery for a term of 14 years, but they included a clause that, if the land was required for railway purposes, the agreement could be terminated by giving six months' notice. This land was not required and so the agreement ran the full 14 years.

The line was on a level elevation from the Old Hall to Liversedge, so that it could pass under what was then known as the Leeds to Huddersfield turnpike road, but now known as the A62. From Liversedge, where reasonable facilities were provided for both goods and passenger traffic, the line climbed the Spen Valley at various gradients of up to 1 in 85, and, clinging to the side of the valley as far as Cleckheaton, most of this was through shallow cuttings and small embankments.

At the site of Cleckheaton station and goods yard the valley side is quite steep, so the contractors had to build a largely one-sided embankment which made a plateau for the railway to sit on. It was also necessary to build a very high road viaduct to provide access to the station and goods yard. The goods yard was quite large and boasted a warehouse, tipping dock, cattle pen and two signal boxes to control the access.

Leaving Cleckheaton, the line swung to the east before entering Gomersal tunnel, which was built of blue engineering brick throughout apart from the stone portals at each end. The tunnel's east end carried the date 1899 in stone numerals and was straight, 819 yds long and with only one ventilation shaft. Being a short, straight, shallow tunnel it was cold, draughty and wet for platelaying gang No. 26 to work in. As there was not much ground above the tunnel, large amounts of water came through the brickwork during wet weather, and, if it was exceptionally cold, this water would freeze, making it necessary for the platelayers to hack away the ice, which could be up to one foot thick, from the tunnel walls.

Adjacent to the eastern portal of this tunnel was Gomersal goods yard and station, which was of timber construction. A subway was also constructed allowing access to the other platform; a similar facility being incorporated at the stations of Cleckheaton and Upper Birstal. The size of the goods yard was not impressive but the warehouse boasted the title "largest of the line", mainly due to its construction utilizing existing buildings. This had previously been used as a textile "willeying" shed, known locally as "The Silk Mill" and later in its life (when the railway company had no need for

# L.N.W.R. LIVERSEDGE

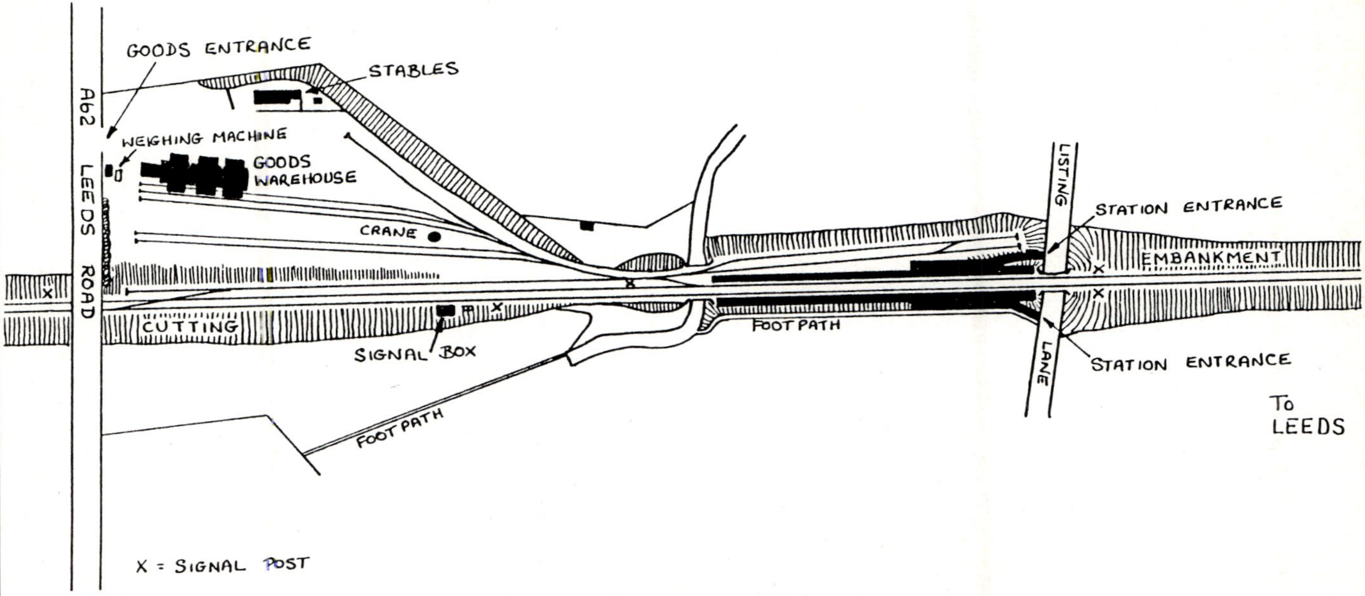


*Redrawn from the 1908 Ordnance Survey Map.*

Stanier '5MT' "Black Five" No. 44780 should have plenty of power to spare on this stopping service about to depart Liversedge Spen for Leeds. *Roy Brook*

This viaduct carries the access road to Cleckheaton station and goods yard. *Author*

# L.N.W.R. CLECKHEATON

*Redrawn from the 1908 Ordnance Survey Map.*

# L.N.W.R. GOMERSAL

--- GOMERSAL TUNNEL.

X = SIGNAL POST

TO LEEDS

EMBANKMENT

NUTTER LANE

GOMERSAL BRIDGE

BRADFORD ROAD

WEIGHING MACHINE

BRADFORD ROAD.

MOOR LANE

STATION ENTRANCE

CRANE

SIGNAL BOX

*Redrawn from the 1908 Ordnance Survey Map.*

## THE ROUTE DESCRIBED                                             41

such a large building) it reverted back to a manufacturing place in the form of a soap works, finishing its life in the hands of a scrap metal merchant.

Some local traders made good use of the goods yard, these included the coal merchants W. Booker, L. Rhodes and W. Schofield, plus the Gomersal textile firm of Thomas Burnley who used the yard for some of their raw material deliveries.

From Gomersal the line made a slight deviation to travel round the perimeter of the grounds of Oakwell Hall at Birstall, where a small aqueduct was provided to channel a water course named Nova Beck. Oakwell Hall has past associations with the Brontë family, and is now the nucleus of a country park, being developed by Kirklees Metropolitan Council.

At a gradient of 1 in 80, the line climbed through a deep cutting to the site of Upper Birstal station and was the area where the contractors Baldry & Yerburgh encountered hard rock. An unusual feature was that Fieldhead Lane bridge at one end was a three-arch blue brick structure, while Raikes Lane bridge at the other end was built of stone, to the same design as most of the bridges at Heckmondwike.

Birstall was where the line reached its highest elevation so from here it was all downhill to Leeds. Passing through a cutting at Howden Clough, the line was crossed first by a three-arch bridge (built of blue brick) which carried a farm road, then a steel bridge which carried the Great Northern line from Bradford to Dewsbury, and finally, Nab Lane which crossed the line on a very lofty stone bridge.

Descending on a gradient of 1 in 70 the line passed through Gildersome tunnel, which, incidentally, burrowed beneath the Great Northern Bradford to Wakefield line (via Morley). Similar to Gomersal tunnel, it was built entirely of blue engineering brick with stone portals at each end. At the time of closure, British Railways quoted its length as 1 mile 571 yds but LNWR records have it as 1 mile 579 yds. With no way of knowing which length is the more accurate, it is more interesting to say that it is "139 tablets" long. Set into the tunnel wall on the down side are numbered tablets spaced at 50 ft intervals, No. 1 being at the Birstall end.

The tunnel was originally built with three ventilation shafts but early in its life the shaft nearest the Birstall end was capped and made blind, but an internal examination chamber was accessible from the inside until the time the tunnel closed in 1965.

It was quite a spacious place in terms of tunnel clearances and platelaying gang No. 28, whose job was to work within the tunnel, did not need to seek a man-refuge if a train passed, they simply stood against the tunnel wall. Being deep and long and 175 ft below ground level (at its deepest) it was much dryer and warmer than the one at Gomersal. At the north end of the tunnel a water course had to be re-routed, this was channelled down a timber chute into a culvert. In the years immediately after nationalization, about 1950, the timber chute was replaced with a concrete pipe.

While on the subject of platelayers, this line was maintained by gangs (of four men) numbered 20 to 29. Gangs 24 and 25 (in the Liversedge and Cleckheaton areas) were amalgamated in 1938 but the gang numbers changed after nationalization and Gildersome East became gang 877.

L.N.W.R. UPPER BIRSTAL
*RENAMED* BIRSTALL TOWN 1935

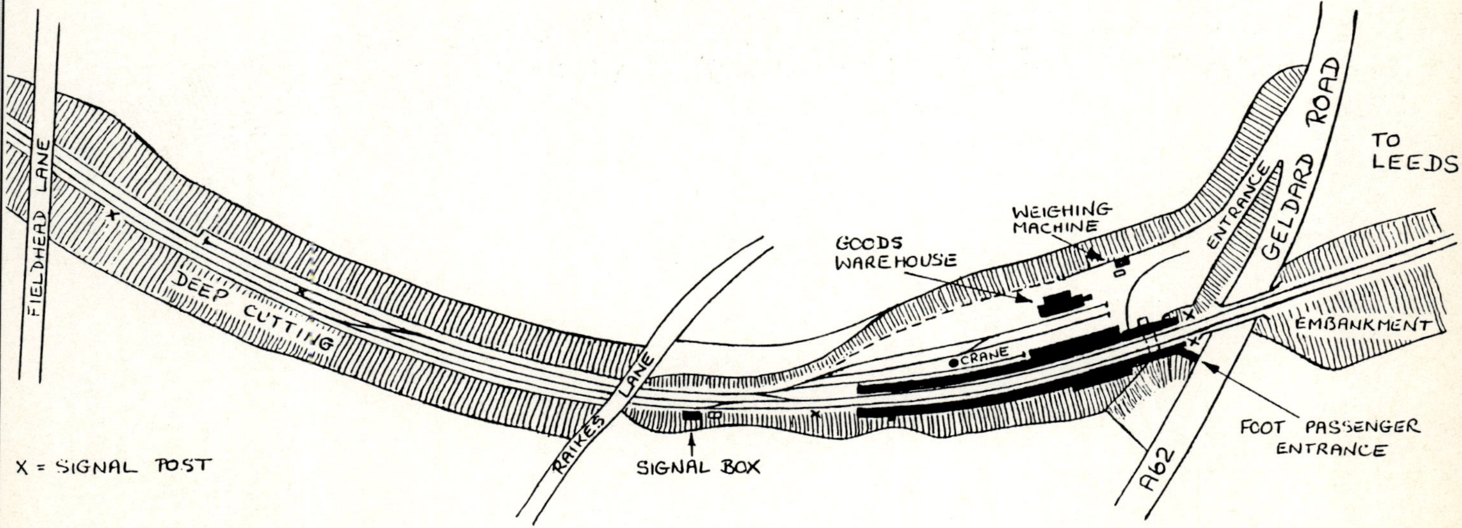


Redrawn from the 1908 Ordnance Survey Map.

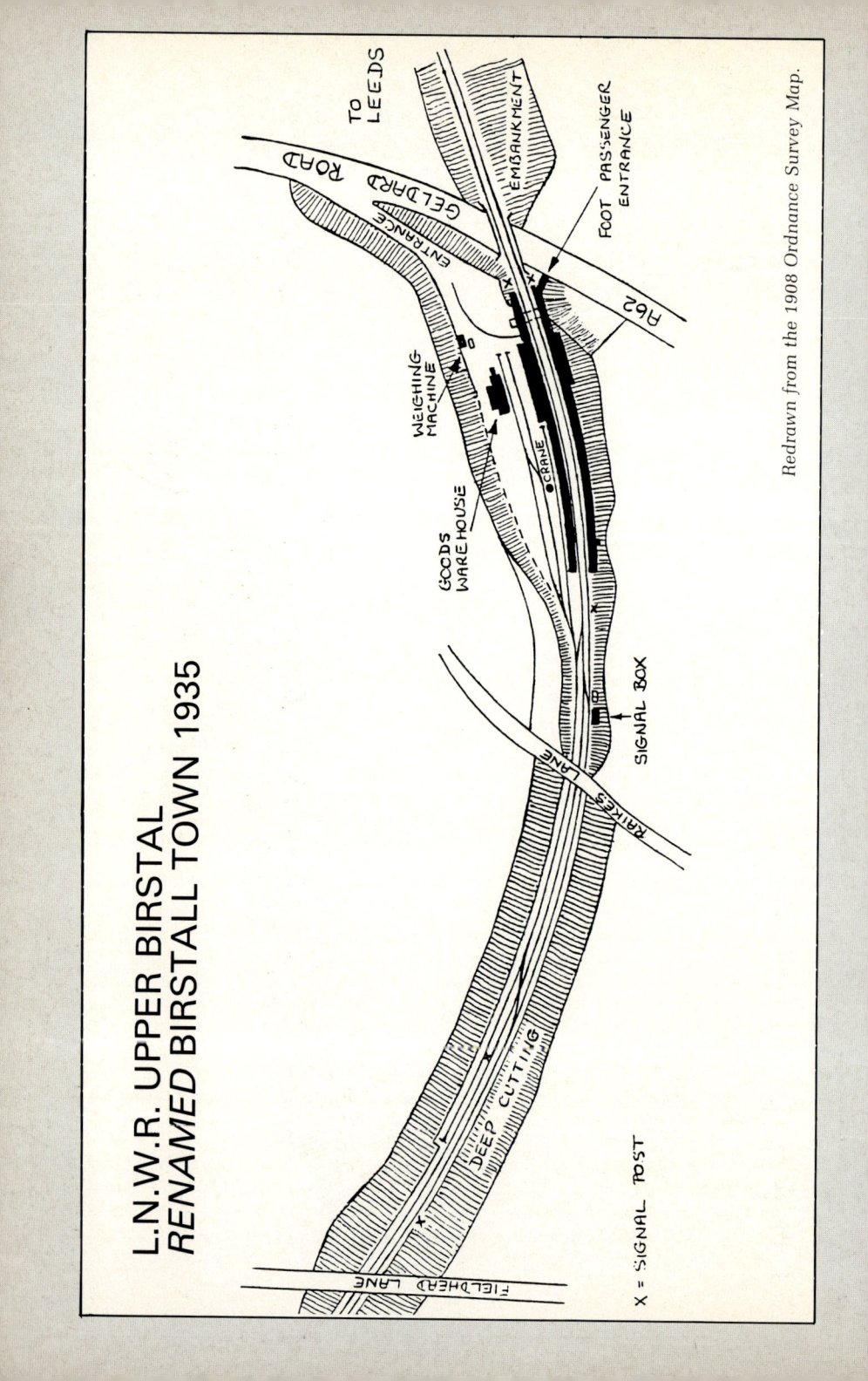

# L.N.W.R. GILDERSOME

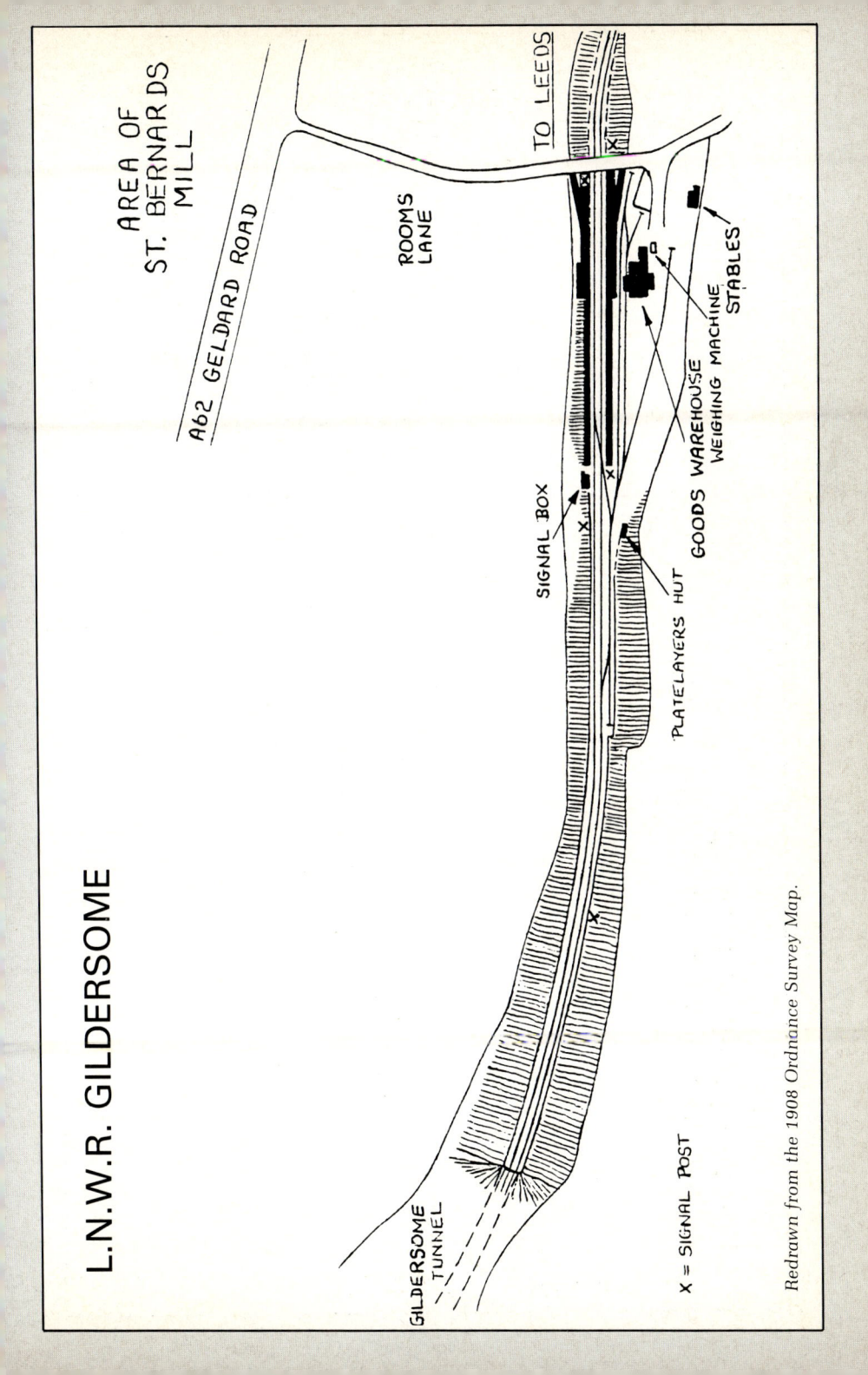

AREA OF ST. BERNARDS MILL

A62 GELDARD ROAD

ROOMS LANE

TO LEEDS

SIGNAL BOX

PLATELAYERS HUT

GOODS WAREHOUSE

WEIGHING MACHINE

STABLES

GILDERSOME TUNNEL

X = SIGNAL POST

*Redrawn from the 1908 Ordnance Survey Map.*

From the north end of Gildersome tunnel it was only a short distance to the station and goods yard. This station was wrongly placed, because apart from a few cottages in Rooms Lane, most people from the township had to walk over one mile to catch the trains. This remote location ensured that most inhabitants did not use this station. The goods yard was provided with a warehouse and stables but was the only station not to possess a yard crane.

There was a mill situated at the end of Rooms Lane in Geldard Road called St Bernard's, so to local people the station was known as Gildersome St Bernard's to distinguish it from the Great Northern station at Gildersome. This station was, however, more conveniently sited to serve the town. Where the LNWR did score over the GN was that the latter did not have a direct service to Leeds, passengers having to travel by a more circuitous route to reach the city.

From Gildersome the line was carried on a high embankment to reach the impressive flying junction at Farnley. Here it rejoined the Leeds to Huddersfield (via Dewsbury) line, which it left at Heaton Lodge.

The line from Huddersfield to Leeds was designated "down" and from Leeds to Huddersfield the "up" line.

Due to the heavily graded nature of the line, catch points were positioned at various places along the route.

*Down Line*
Battyeford & Mirfield – 318 yds on the Huddersfield side of the Battyeford & Mirfield down distant signal.
Liversedge – 396 yds on the Huddersfield side of Liversedge down home No. 1 signal.
Cleckheaton – 387 yds on the Huddersfield side of Cleckheaton No. 1 down home and No. 2 down distant signal.
Gomersal Tunnel – 368 yds on the Huddersfield side of the mouth of Gomersal Tunnel.
Upper Birstal – 400 yds on the Huddersfield side of Upper Birstal down home signal.

*Up Line*
Gildersome – 409 yds on the Leeds side of Gildersome up home signal.
Farnley & Wortley – 199 yds on the Leeds side of Farnley Junction up line advance starting signal.

All these catch points were self-acting except the one at Farnley & Wortley which could also be worked from the signal box.

The construction and permanent way work was completed, except for the passenger and goods stations, towards the end of July 1900, bringing the total length of the line to approximately 13$7/16$ miles. The down line to Leeds was just over ¾ mile shorter than the up line to Huddersfield mainly due to the construction of the flying junction at Farnley.

The line descends from Gildersome for most of the way at a gradient of 1 in 70, with 220 yds or so at 1 in 52, whereas the line to Huddersfield had a less severe gradient of 1 in 80 to be climbed, because of its extra length.

The north end of Gildersome tunnel showing the timber water chute which was later to be replaced with a concrete pipe.  *Real Photographs*

The same view as above but in 1985.  *Author*

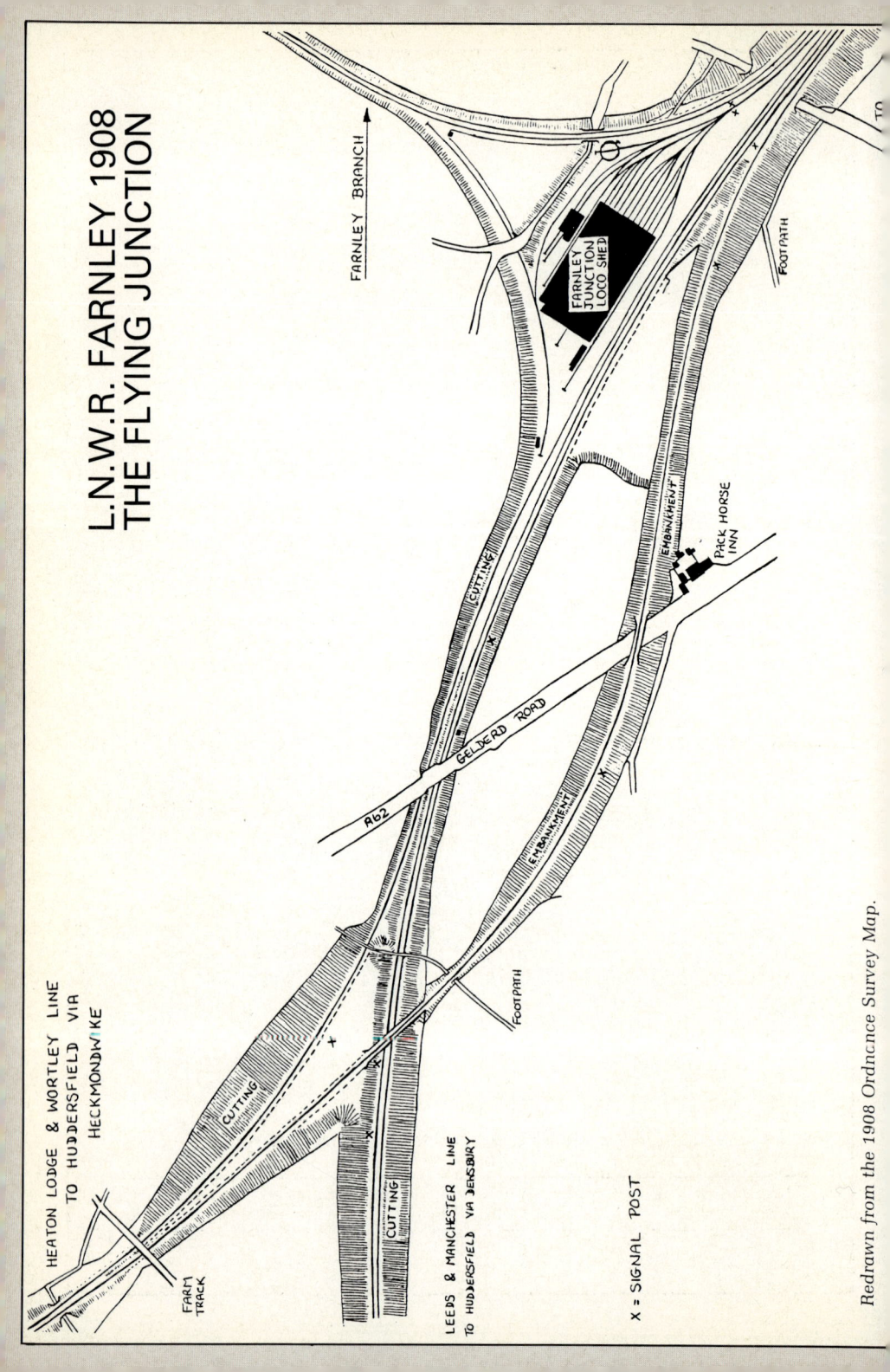

# L.N.W.R. FARNLEY 1908
## THE FLYING JUNCTION

*Redrawn from the 1908 Ordnance Survey Map.*

## LNWR GRADIENT TABLE

| Distance from Heckmondwike Junction in miles From | To | Rising or Falling R | F | Gradient 1 in | Location |
|---|---|---|---|---|---|
| 0 | – | 1/16 | | | Level | Heckmondwike Junction and Battyeford |
| 1/16 | – | 3/8 | | F | 105 | ,, |
| | at | 3/8 | | F | 500 | ,, |
| 3/8 | – | 7/16 | | | Level | ,, |
| 7/16 | – | 11/16 | R | | 90 | ,, |
| 11/16 | – | 7/8 | R | | 230 | ,, |
| 7/8 | – | 15/16 | | | Level | ,, |
| 15/16 | – | 1 1/8 | R | | 85 | ,, |
| 1 1/8 | – | 1 1/4 | R | | 260 | At Battyeford & Mirfield station |
| 1 1/4 | – | 1 9/16 | R | | 85 | Battyeford & Mirfield and Northorpe |
| 1 9/16 | – | 1 5/8 | R | | 88 | ,, |
| 1 5/8 | – | 1 11/16 | | | Level | ,, |
| 1 11/16 | – | 1 7/8 | | F | 176 | ,, |
| 1 7/8 | – | 1 15/16 | | | Level | ,, |
| 1 15/16 | – | 2 1/16 | R | | 550 | ,, |
| 2 1/16 | – | 2 3/16 | R | | 100 | ,, |
| 2 3/16 | – | 2 1/4 | | | Level | ,, |
| 2 1/4 | – | 2 7/16 | | F | 200 | ,, |
| 2 7/16 | – | 2 9/16 | | F | 275 | ,, |
| 2 9/16 | – | 2 13/16 | | | Level | Northorpe and Heckmondwike |
| 2 13/16 | – | 3 1/4 | | F | 340 | ,, |
| 3 1/4 | – | 3 5/16 | | | Level | ,, |
| 3 5/16 | – | 3 1/2 | R | | 178 | ,, |
| 3 1/2 | – | 3 13/16 | R | | 578 | ,, |
| 3 13/16 | – | 3 7/8 | | F | 120 | ,, |
| 3 7/8 | – | 4 1/8 | R | | 90 | ,, |
| 4 1/8 | – | 4 3/8 | R | | 260 | At Heckmondwike station |
| 4 3/8 | – | 4 11/16 | R | | 108 | Heckmondwike and Liversedge |
| 4 11/16 | – | 4 7/8 | | | Level | ,, |
| 4 7/8 | – | 5 1/16 | R | | 85 | ,, |
| 5 1/16 | – | 5 3/16 | R | | 260 | At Liversedge station |
| 5 3/16 | – | 6 1/16 | R | | 85 | Liversedge and Cleckheaton |
| | at | 6 1/16 | | | Level | ,, |
| 6 1/16 | – | 6 3/16 | | F | 260 | At Cleckheaton station |
| 6 3/16 | – | 6 1/4 | | | Level | Cleckheaton and Gomersal |
| 6 1/4 | – | 6 7/16 | R | | 260 | ,, |
| 6 7/16 | – | 7 9/16 | R | | 77 | ,, |
| 7 9/16 | – | 7 7/8 | R | | 260 | Gomersal and Upper Birstal |
| 7 7/8 | – | 8 3/4 | R | | 80 | ,, |
| 8 3/4 | – | 9 1/8 | R | | 260 | Upper Birstal and Gildersome tunnel |
| 9 1/8 | – | 9 1/4 | | | Level | ,, |
| 9 1/4 | – | 9 1/2 | | F | 90 | ,, |
| 9 1/2 | – | 10 | | F | 121 | ,, |
| 10 | – | 13 3/8 | | F | 70 | Gildersome tunnel and Farnley Junction |
| 13 3/8 | – | 13 7/16 | | F | 80 | ,, |
| 12 1/2 | – | 12 15/16 | | F | 52 | ⎱ Gildersome and Farnley Junction |
| 12 15/16 | – | 13 7/16 | | F | 100 | ⎰ Down line only through the flying junction |

Two views of the timber station at Gomersal looking towards Leeds. The down line signal is fitted to the up line post to give drivers an earlier sighting when emerging from Gomersal tunnel as the line was on a curve. This was one of only three stations on the line to be provided with a subway. The goods yard is to the right of the scene.
*(Both) Lens of Sutton*

Upper Birstal station showing the typical timber structure as used by the LNWR. Taken in the early part of the century and looking towards Huddersfield, it demonstrates many facets of station life.
*G.S. Cooper*

The exterior of Upper Birstal station from Geldard Road looking towards Leeds in the early 1900s. Plainly on view is the timber staircase roofed with corrugated iron. This station was provided with a passenger subway with the entrance about half way up the staircase.
*G.S. Cooper*

This early photograph of Gildersome signal box shows that the station platform construction was timber decking supported on a brick base.  *David K. Atkinson*

# Chapter Four
## The Early Years

Colonel Yorke and Major Pringle inspected the line on behalf of the Board of Trade on 30th and 31st July respectively, and, subject to a few requirements in connection with signals, approval was received thus allowing the line to be opened for through freight trains on 1st August.

An inspection party consisting of Directors and chief officials of the LNWR visited the line on 12th September.

It was said that every effort would be made to complete the passenger stations, so that the line could be fully operational from the official opening date of 1st October, 1900.

Although the line was operational, a few outstanding requirements still needed completion. The company had to pay an acknowledgement of 1s. per annum to Mr J. Fearnley in respect of windows in a house and warehouse overlooking Moor Lane at Gomersal. It also had to pay £125 to the trustees of the late John Day for interfering with lights on their property in Geldard Road (known as Lambsfield Buildings) during construction of the railway.

The line was due to be opened on the 9th July, 1900, for goods traffic only but during the month of June there were still considerable permanent way and contractors' personnel working between Heckmondwike and Birstall. To make matters worse the line had its first railway accident before it even opened.

As in most railway accidents a strange sequence of events caused the mishap. The sequence commenced with a workmen's train, which ran from Hillhouse at Huddersfield at about the same time every morning. This travelled as far as was necessary each day to drop off workmen along the line, at their places of work, usually terminating at Upper Birstal. During the month of June, the northern part of the line had been ballasted from a staithe near Farnley which had become exhausted on 28th June, so arrangements were made to run only one train to pick up ballast at Northorpe on the morning of 29th June. On this particular morning the workmen's train, consisting of 0–6–0 locomotive No. 1735 (running tender first) a third class brake coach, two open wagons and a goods brake, left Hillhouse at Huddersfield as usual to pick up and drop men off along the line at Battyeford, Northorpe, Heckmondwike and Cleckheaton where it arrived at 6.40 am. The train travelled on the correct (down) line until Cleckheaton. This particular morning the contractors had a train operating on this line between Cleckheaton and Gomersal, so single line working was in operation over the up line with a flag man travelling on the train which had authority to proceed.

Meanwhile the ballast train had started from Farnley Junction at about 6.00 am and consisted of goods locomotive No. 1233, fifteen empty wagons and two brake vans. This train travelled "wrong line" to Upper Birstal and the instructions were that it was to be met by a flag man. Unfortunately, when it arrived, there was no flag man present so the guard told the driver to proceed to Gomersal, where it was crossed over to the up line to avoid the contractors' train working between Cleckheaton and Gomersal.

The workmen's train, which was at Cleckheaton, had now been crossed to the up line and was departing for Gomersal. Near No. 2 signal box the driver saw the ballast train coming into view, rounding the curve under Cliffe Lane bridge some 100 yds or so away and travelling at a smart pace. He immediately threw his locomotive into reverse, which alerted the workmen to the impending disaster and most of them luckily jumped off. At the point of impact both trains had managed to slow down to about 5 or 6 mph, but in the event three men were seriously injured with a further 16 receiving minor injuries. The tender of the workmen's train suffered extensive damage but the ballast train locomotive only suffered a broken buffer.

On Wednesday 8th August Major General Hutchinson, representing the Board of Trade, opened an enquiry at Cleckheaton Town Hall into the collision on 29th June. It transpired that the ballast train should have waited at Upper Birstal for the flagman to arrive who apparently was travelling with the workmen's train. Both trains were then to return as one, to Northorpe. The blame lay with the guard of the ballast train for misunderstanding his instructions, but there was doubt as to whether the instructions had been clearly given.

The strange sequence of events which culminated in the accident were summed up as:

1. The staithe at Farnley becoming exhausted on 28th June.
2. The guard of the ballast train misunderstanding his instructions.
3. The ballast train driver was a new man unfamiliar with the working of the line.
4. A contractor's train working on the line that particular morning, making single line working necessary.
5. The company had chosen to run the ballast train then knowing that there would be a workmen's train at that time of day.

If any one of these factors had been different then the accident would probably not have occurred.

The line and all the stations were officially opened to passengers on Monday 1st October, 1900; there was no official ceremony, but officials of the LNWR did travel over the line throughout the day. At the same time the goods stations at Gomersal, Upper Birstal and Gildersome were opened to local freight with two goods trains each day stopping to pick up traffic. Because they were not completed, the goods stations at Heckmondwike, Liversedge and Cleckheaton did not officially open until Thursday 1st November.

Coaching stock to the equivalent of four trains was specially built for use over the new line. Electric lighting was fitted, power being supplied from a dynamo driven from the axle of the guard's van (where all the switches were fitted) to be under the control of the guard at all times. This facility must have been very beneficial to passengers in view of the various tunnels, especially at a time when gas lighting was still widespread.

The new line attracted considerable local interest on the first day. Every station experienced large numbers of people buying a return ticket to the next station just for the fun of it, and to sample the new railway for themselves.

# THE EARLY YEARS 53

A typical LNWR freight locomotive of class 'G2' trundles past Cleckheaton Spen in 1950 with a mixed freight heading towards Huddersfield. *Author's Collection*

Sunday peacefulness is shattered in August 1949, as "Black Five" No. 44782, piloting an unrebuilt "Royal Scot", pass stored coaching stock at Cleckheaton Spen with a diverted Liverpool-bound express. *Author's Collection*

The LNWR was experimenting at this period with an issue of what they called "Market Tickets" so these tickets were made available on Wednesdays and Saturdays for certain return journeys to Leeds, at a very reduced price.

During the first day of operation over 800 tickets were issued at the Heckmondwike station alone but being a market town with over 9,000 inhabitants this is not really surprising. At Gomersal where the township was not much bigger than village proportions, bookings exceeded all expectations with the following ticket sales being recorded during the first month.

Ticket Sales at Gomersal

| 15 | to Manchester | 118½ | to Huddersfield |
| 7 | to Bradley | 28 | to Battyeford & Mirfield |
| 38½ | to Northorpe | 237 | to Heckmondwike |
| 164 | to Liversedge | 1129½ | to Cleckheaton |
| 448½ | to Upper Birstal | 45 | to Gildersome |
| 77½ | to Farnley & Wortley | 792½ | to Leeds |
| 307½ | to Leeds (Market) | 2 | to Rugby |
| 2 | to Blackpool (Weekend) | 3 | to New Brighton (Weekend) |
| 2 | to Morcambe (Weekend) | | |

The large number of bookings to Cleckheaton is probably because vast numbers of people made a journey on the first day of operation for the ride only.

*Tickets*

Certain arrangements were made so that some tickets were interchangeable with stations on the Huddersfield to Leeds line (via Dewsbury).

Both single and return tickets to places via Huddersfield were available:
1. Gildersome or Morley – at either of those places.
2. Upper Birstal, Birstal, Carlinghow and Batley – at any one of those places but passengers made their own way between Birstal and Upper Birstal stations.
3. Northorpe or Ravensthorpe & Thornhill – at either of those places.
4. Battyeford & Mirfield or Mirfield – at either of those places.

Return halves of tickets were available as follows:
1. Leeds and Huddersfield with – Gildersome or Morley at either of those places.
2. Leeds and Huddersfield with – Battyeford & Mirfield or Mirfield at either of those places.
3. Leeds with – Northorpe at Ravensthorpe & Thornhill.
4. Leeds with – Batley, Carlinghow, Birstal to return via Upper Birstal.
5. Huddersfield with – Northorpe or Ravensthorpe & Thornhill at either of those places.
6. Huddersfield with – Upper Birstal, Birstal, Carlinghow and Batley at any one of those places.

*Note*

   Birstal and Carlinghow stations were on the short LNWR terminus branch from Batley, known to local people as the "Coddy Bob" line.

In October 1900 it was apparent that the £1 float balance allocated to Heckmondwike was insufficient as in December this was increased to £2,

# THE EARLY YEARS

followed in February 1901 by Cleckheaton, Upper Birstal (October 1901) and Battyeford & Mirfield in May 1902. It appears that the stations at Northorpe, Liversedge, Gomersal and Gildersome remained at £1, although this was increased to £2 at Gomersal in February 1920.

A decision was taken on 14th November, 1900 to adopt a permanent issue of "Market Tickets" from Northorpe to Leeds costing 1s. 4d. This was quickly followed by a similar issue from Battyeford & Mirfield to Leeds costing 1d. less at 1s. 3d. Keeping a keen eye on sales, the Heckmondwike U.D.C. and Tradesmen's Association applied to the company in June 1901, asking them to adopt "Market Fares" to Heckmondwike. It was agreed to introduce the following fares:

| Battyeford & Mirfield | to | Heckmondwike | 4d. |
| Upper Birstal | to | Heckmondwike | 6d. |
| Gomersal | to | Heckmondwike | 5d. |
| Cleckheaton | to | Heckmondwike | 3d. |

The only other market town of reasonable size which the line served was Cleckheaton, and, not wishing to be left out, the Cleckheaton U.D.C. applied to the company on 19th March, 1902 for Market fares to be adopted on Saturdays only.

It was subsequently agreed to adopt the following:

| Upper Birstal | to | Cleckheaton | 4d. |
| Gomersal | to | Cleckheaton | 2d. |
| Northorpe | to | Cleckheaton | 5d. |
| Battyeford & Mirfield | to | Cleckheaton | 7d. |

A selection of Standard fares from Cleckheaton during October 1900 was as follows:

| To | Type of Ticket | First Class | Second Class | Third Class |
| --- | --- | --- | --- | --- |
| Huddersfield | Single | 1s. 7d. | 11d. | 9½d. |
| Huddersfield | Return | 2s. 8d. | 1s. 6d. | 1s. 4d. |
| Leeds | Single | 1s. 6d. | 11d. | 9½d. |
| Leeds | Return | 2s. 10d. | 1s. 9d. | 1s. 7d. |

Staffing levels for working the new line were classed as temporary at first but were made permanent in January 1902 at the following levels:

### COACHING

*Heckmondwike Junction*
   3 signalmen – Rate of pay 26/-, 27/- &
     28/- per week

*Battyeford & Mirfield*
   1 station master – Max. £90 per annum
   1 porter – (relief signalman)
   1 junior porter
   1 junior parcels porter
   2 signalmen

### GOODS

1 goods agent – Max. £140 per annum
1 goods clerk – Max. £80 per annum
1 apprentice clerk
1 foreman
2 carters
2 adult porters
1 weigher

*Northorpe*
- 1 station master – Max. £80 per annum
- 1 junior porter
- 1 porter – signalman

*Heckmondwike*
- 1 station master – Max. £120 per annum
- 1 apprentice clerk
- 1 parcel vanman
- 2 porter-signalmen
- 2 signalmen – (Goods Box)
- 1 signalman – (Goods Box and Battyeford & Mirfield)
- 1 goods agent – Max. £180 per annum
- 1 goods clerk – Max. £100 per annum
- 1 goods clerk – Max. £80 per annum
- 1 apprentice clerk
- 1 warehouse foreman & townsman
- 2 porters or warehousemen
- 1 tranship guard
- 1 weigher
- 1 stable foreman & carter
- 4 carters

*Liversedge*
- 1 station master – Max. £100 per annum
- 1 apprentice
- 1 porter (relief signalman)
- 1 junior porter
- 2 signalmen
- 1 goods clerk – Max. £80 per annum
- 1 weigher
- 1 foreman and townsman
- 2 carters
- 1 adult porter
- 1 junior porter
- 1 chain lad

*Cleckheaton*
- 1 station master – Max. £110 per annum
- 1 apprentice clerk
- 1 porter (relief signalman)
- 1 shunter
- 1 junior porter
- 5 signalmen (Nos. 1 & 2 cabins)
- 1 goods clerk – Max. £90 per annum
- 2 apprentice clerks
- 1 foreman townsman
- 4 carters
- 2 porters
- 1 chain lad

*Gomersal*
- 1 station master & goods agent – Max. £100 per annum
- 1 apprentice clerk
- 1 porter (relief signalman)
- 2 signalmen
- 1 apprentice clerk
- 1 foreman
- 1 two-horse carter

*Upper Birstal*
- 1 station master – Max. £90 per annum
- 1 apprentice clerk
- 1 porter (relief signalman)
- 2 signalmen
- 1 check clerk

*Gildersome*
- 1 station master – Max. £80 per annum
- 2 signalmen
- 1 signalman (working between Gildersome & Upper Birstal)
- 1 carter
- 1 goods porter

*Farnley & Wortley Junction*
- 2 train recorders

This view of Heckmondwike station, taken during the early part of the century, shows a variation of the platform canopy to that used at other stations on the line.

*Douglas Hird*

The cannon in Sparrow Park dates this photograph of the LNWR station about 1920, before it was renamed Heckmondwike Spen.   *Author's Collection*

Passenger services started with what can best be described as a "reasonable frequency", the timetable showing twelve trains in each direction on weekdays but no Sunday service. The average journey time was approximately one hour, this being reduced by 5 minutes or so on services which did not stop at Farnley & Wortley or Bradley. These two stations were also served by the Huddersfield to Leeds via Dewsbury services.

1902 saw the addition of an extra train on Saturdays only, departing Leeds at 1.10 pm calling at all stations to Heckmondwike (where it terminated) returning at 2.30 pm with a similar service to Leeds. This train ran until 1906 when it was extended through to Huddersfield, with an extra train from Huddersfield at 1.50 pm to cover the service back to Leeds. Heckmondwike was the only station on the line to be provided with a bay platform and this was situated at the Leeds end of the station. Late night journeys were altered in 1902 to run Wednesday and Saturday only and one can presume that there could not have been any demand on the other days.

During the early months of operation some problems arose connected with operating practice. In April 1901 it was considered necessary to construct a tipping dock at Liversedge at an estimated cost of £600. It was also found to be necessary in October 1901 to provide a footbridge at Battyeford & Mirfield passenger station and this work (along with another footbridge) was put out to tender. The company accepted a tender from Messrs Butler & Company to construct both bridges at a total cost of £938. By February 1902, two pairs of hand operated points in the shunting yard at Cleckheaton were proving to be troublesome, so it was decided to connect these to No. 2 signal box at an estimated cost of £29.

During March 1902 the contractors Baldry & Yerburgh entered a claim for £113,000 against the company for extras arising out of their contract for the Wortley section. The company refused to pay this exorbitant amount, and, although the LNWR's Chief Engineer had the right to arbitrate, it was considered advisable to call in an independent engineer. Sir J. Wolfe Barry accepted this request and advised the company to offer a lump sum in settlement. The Chief Engineer and solicitor were instructed to agree a settlement at no more than £40,000, this was rejected by the contractors in June 1903, but by August 1903 the contractor's solicitors agreed to accept £45,000, which was acceptable to the LNWR and the claim was thankfully settled.

The ledger for the Heaton Lodge and Wortley Railway was finally closed on 30th June, 1906 by which time the total cost had risen to £1,052,579 13s. 10d.

The 1906 service remained basically unaltered until it was drastically cut back to meet wartime conditions in 1914 to seven trains each way (with one extra service on Saturdays).

This very austere service was endured until 1st October, 1919, when the Saturdays only lunch time service commenced running daily. A late night service was reintroduced departing Leeds at 11 pm on Wednesdays and Saturdays only.

Heckmondwike cutting in LNWR days taken from about the end of the station; it shows the siding to the bay platform. *Real Photographs*

Heckmondwike Old Hall in relation to the railway. It also shows how a portion of one wing was sliced off. The Heckmondwike distant signal was sited against the first bridge with a white board behind it until the 1960s resignalling of the line, when the old lower quadrant was replaced with this more modern upper quadrant. *Author*

"Carter" John Hosley with one of the company's horses at Cleckheaton Spen stables during the early part of the century. *Alan S. Bagot*

The LMS introduced the "Hawkseye" station nameboard in 1937 so this photograph of Cleckheaton Spen station, looking in the direction of Liversedge, is probably from the post-war period. It was the only station to be provided with a subway large enough for small vehicles, which would originally be horse drawn. *Douglas Hird*

The following statement, issued by the Railway Executive during April 1919, may indicate the reason why passenger services were not increased to pre-war levels.

> In view of the serious difficulties of the railway companies in providing engines and rolling stock for the conveyance of traffic, it is desirable that the public should be acquainted with the problems caused by the war, and their effect on the holiday traffic of 1919. Soon after the outbreak of war, the railway companies placed the whole of their workshops at the disposal of the War Minister for the manufacture of munitions, and for the last four years only the minimum amount of repairs to engines and rolling stock has been carried out. The result of this effort in the national interest is that the companies are left with practically all their engines in need of overhauling, and thousands of passenger coaches unfit for running. Of the 700 engines and many trains sent to France and other theatres of war, practically none has as yet been returned. It is obvious that four years arrears in repairs cannot be made good by the summer. The Railway Executive Committee wish to point out that if, following the usual practice, the bulk of the holidays are taken in July and August, there will be difficulty in coping with the traffic. If, however, those who are able to do so will take their holidays in May and June, this will do much to obviate any overcrowding and discomfort that might otherwise arise. It is particularly urged that Tuesdays, Wednesdays, Thursdays and Fridays should be used for holiday travelling as on these days the traffic is usually lighter.

The company's goods warehouses at Heckmondwike, Liversedge and Cleckheaton were all very similar structures being built of timber. They were about 40 yds long by 10 yds wide, with an annexe at one end which was the office. The timber structure proved to be the undoing of the Heckmondwike warehouse, as it was razed to the ground by fire on the evening of 17th November, 1915.

Apparently, a lorry owned by The Co-operative Wholesale Society which had been delivering a load of boots and shoes, was being filled with petrol from a can when spillage on to the hot exhaust caused this to ignite. Because the lorry was parked at the loading dock, the fire quickly spread to the warehouse structure. The goods agent, Mr Hodgson, and his staff tried to control the fire with extinguishers, but by the time the fire brigade arrived, the building was well alight. Within half an hour of the outbreak the roof and walls had collapsed in a mass of flame. The lorry was completely destroyed in the inferno, but the firemen did manage to save the warehouse office, although the company's books had been moved to a safer place.

The Heckmondwike warehouse was never rebuilt, its business being transferred to Liversedge, which was just over a mile down the line at the other end of town. Fourteen months later on 17th January, 1917, the Co-operative Wholesale Society offered £1,125 compensation for the destruction of the warehouse, and this was accepted.

A brief statement was issued in July 1917 to the effect that Gildersome "St Bernard's" station would close on 1st August until further notice. It was one of a number of stations closed during World War I as an economy measure but was the only station on the Heaton Lodge and Wortley Line to be so affected.

After the war hostilities had ceased, a deputation from Gildersome

Council had a meeting with officials of the LNWR with a view to the re-opening of "St Bernard's" station. The company pointed out that owing to the reduced quantity of goods traffic and the small amount of passenger traffic on offer, they could not see their way to re-open the station, but made the concession that, should the council require material for repairing the approach roads, arrangements would be made to have this left at the station.

It was not until May 1919 that Gildersome Council received a letter from the LNWR stating that "St Bernard's" station had been re-opened from 5th May for both goods and passenger traffic, but with a much reduced frequency of service to that which existed before the war.

April 1920 saw the owners of St Bernard's Mill asking Gildersome Council if they would approach the LNWR with a view to arranging for more trains to stop at "St Bernard's" station. It was pointed out that people could not be expected to use the station with such a poor service offered: only five trains to Leeds and three trains to Huddersfield each weekday. However, this request had no effect because in June 1921 the LNWR decided to close Gildersome station completely on economic grounds. Morley Borough Council asked for the station to be kept open, but were told that the station did not pay its way and would have to close at the start of the next timetable.

The receipts at the station did not pay for half the costs of running it, and the company said that it was costing them about 2s. to stop and start each train. Most of the railway companies resumed a full summer timetable on Monday 11th July, after being released from government control for the period of the war effort. This included the LNWR, so with no Sunday service on this line Gildersome station closed after the last train on Saturday 9th July, 1921.

The honour for the slowest train to travel over the line must surely go to a passenger train which left Huddersfield on the evening of Wednesday 1st October, 1919 and did not arrive in Leeds until mid-morning the following day. Outside Cleckheaton station the train was held on what was said to be a slippery rail, and the passengers had to make their way to the station to continue their journey in taxi cabs. Various rumours were circulated making it appear that the train was a victim of a railway strike which was in progress at the time, but as this was only having a "patchy" effect around the country, this reason did not hold weight.

With 1921 seeing the country in the grip of a miners' strike, some of the railway companies tried to economise on coal consumption by cancelling some of the little used and least important journeys.

Even though coal supplies had come to a halt, the strike was having little or no effect on householders. That summer was so hot and dry that grass and wood had become tinder dry. Temperatures rose to heatwave proportions, the hottest day in Yorkshire was Saturday 9th July with shade temperatures reaching 86°F, while a staggering 125°F was recorded in the sun.

Little did the staff of Northorpe station know what was before them when they started their day's work on Monday 11th July. At about 6 pm on that Monday evening a goods train passed heading in the direction of Huddersfield. Shortly afterwards a grass fire started on the railway embankment some distance away from the station in the direction of Leeds.

This is Northorpe station after the fire damage of July 1921. At the right is the remains of the covered staircase to what was the platform used for trains to Leeds.
*Author's Collection*

Shillbank Lane Northorpe in the vicinity of the station. This view taken prior to 1924 shows the original station name which was later changed to Northorpe Higher.
*J. Fisher*

The fire travelled at an alarming speed towards the station, which it reached in a few minutes, fanned by a light breeze, and it was not long before the timber platforms caught fire.

The station master, Mr Harry Rhymes, was off duty at the time and Mr T. Pearson, porter-signalman, was in charge of the station and raised the alarm. He then raced to the signal box, which was a few hundred yards up the line, to set the signals at danger.

The fire raged with such an intensity that the staff were unable to contain it with their own appliances. The first Fire Brigade to arrive at the burning station was that of Thornton Kelly & Co., cotton spinners from just down the road, followed shortly afterwards by the Mirfield Urban District Fire Brigade.

The firemen had difficulty fighting the fire because the hydrants were between the two blazing platforms, and one of these was found to have no water supply. The station was considered a "lost cause" after half an hour, so the firemen concentrated on saving a row of houses in Eastfield Road, which had their windows broken and woodwork scorched by the intense heat.

The fire spread to the whole length of the station and it was feared that the station buildings would fall backwards onto the houses in Eastfield Road, but the weight of the platform canopy pulled the burning buildings forward onto the track.

A short stretch of about 50 yds at the Heckmondwike end of the down platform was saved by workmen cutting away a stretch of the platform so that the fire could not cross the gap. The fire was not subdued until about 10 pm and continued to smoulder for several hours afterwards.

When the daylight of Tuesday morning broke, it could be seen that the whole station had been burned to the ground, with the exception of the lower part of the two covered approach staircases and the portion of "saved" platform. Among the buildings destroyed were two booking offices, two booking halls and general waiting rooms, four ladies' and gentlemen's first class waiting rooms, a porters' room and the usual other offices on each platform.

The fire had been so fierce that the heat had badly twisted all the track in the vicinity of the station. The down line suffered least and the breakdown gangs succeeded in clearing away the debris and laying a fresh set of metals by 8 am Wednesday morning. Meanwhile trains were worked only as far as Heckmondwike on one side and Battyeford on the other.

The 8.34 am train into Northorpe from Leeds was the first to approach the station and the passengers had to alight onto the side of the track. Through traffic was then possible on a single line.

The weather broke by the end of the same week with thunderstorms over several parts of the country followed by torrential rain.

The station was later rebuilt by the LNWR at an estimated cost of £15,000, but by 1922 the station had lost its importance due to the L&Y being absorbed by the LNWR. This absorption gained for the LNWR the ex-L&Y Northorpe North Road station which also served Huddersfield direct.

During April 1922, the Engineer reported that one of the cast iron girders

## THE EARLY YEARS

Bradshaw's Passenger Timetable for October 1911.

LNWR Passenger Timetable for October 1921.

of the bridge carrying the Leeds to Huddersfield turnpike road over the railway at Liversedge was found to be partially fractured. The width of roadway necessary to take out the girder and the adjoining jack arches was fenced off, and the girder replaced with a second-hand one from company stock at Miles Platting.

The Railways Act of 1921 came into full operation in January 1923. This grouped together individual railway companies into four large groups known as the "Big Four".

The whole of the railway network of the Spen Valley came within the new LMS group and, as each town had more than one station, some changes were deemed necessary.

The stations on the Heaton Lodge and Wortley line at Heckmondwike, Liversedge and Cleckheaton had the word "Spen" added to the name, although this did not appear in timetables until July 1924. This made a clear distinction from the ex-L&Y stations, which were known as "Central".

The station at Battyeford, which until then had been called Battyeford & Mirfield, had the word Mirfield removed and was known simply as Battyeford. This was to avoid confusion with the ex-L&Y station which had served the town of Mirfield for almost 80 years. The LNWR station at Northorpe was named Northorpe Higher to avoid confusion with the ex-L&Y Northorpe North Road.

The only other conflicting name was Heckmondwike Junction at Heaton Lodge. As there was a junction on the ex-L&Y Railway at Heckmondwike, the junction of the Heaton Lodge and Wortley line was renamed Spen Valley Junction.

An unfortunate accident happened at Heckmondwike Spen station on Tuesday 13th February, 1923. At about five minutes past six the 5.40 am train from Leeds was arriving, when a passenger alighted before the train had come to a standstill. The passenger slipped on the wood step of the carriage and fell down between the train and the platform, sustaining severe injuries. Other passengers helped the station staff in rescuing the injured man, who was then sent to hospital where he had to have one arm amputated. Unfortunately he died later the same week from septic poisoning.

At the inquest it was stated that only a few lamps were lit on the platform near to the ticket barrier, and the rest of the station was dark. Fellow passengers who travelled to work on the same train each morning said that the man was a regular traveller who boarded at Farnley & Wortley and was used to getting off at Heckmondwike. But on this particular morning the train appeared to have come to a stop because they could feel no movement. On the day of the accident someone had said that the carriage step was broken, but investigation found this not to be so therefore an accidental verdict was recorded.

At the turn of the century the Lighthouse Chemical Works, in Walkley Lane at Heckmondwike was in the ownership of Greenwoods Tannery. Just prior to 1920 this company was bought by J.C. Oxley and the plant started the manufacture of dyes and chemicals. Part of the premises was used to establish a storage and distribution depot of the National Benzole Association.

The next three pages show the LMS Passenger Timetable down New Line service for September 1936 and its connections.

## WEEK DAYS—continued.

A thin line between the hour and minute figures indicates p.m.

| Station | Saturdays only. | Saturdays excepted. | Saturdays only. | | | | Saturdays only. | | Through Express—London (Euston) to Huddersfield and Halifax. | |
|---|---|---|---|---|---|---|---|---|---|---|
| **Liverpool** (Lime Street) dep. | | | | 12SX0 | | | | 1 0 | | |
| ,, (Exchange) §§ ,, | | | | | | | | | | |
| Llandudno ,, | | | | | | | | 9N40 | | |
| Chester (General) ,, | | | | 10X20 | | | | 11N37 | | |
| Warrington (Bank Quay) ,, | | | | | | | | 12N15 | | |
| Blackpool (North) §§ ,, | | | | 10 45 | | | | 11 15 | | |
| ,, (Central) §§ ,, | | | | | | | | 10 55 | | |
| **Manchester** (Exchange) dep. | | | | 12 50 | | | | 1 45 | | |
| Ashton (Charlestown) | | | | 1 5 | | | | 1 58 | | |
| Stalybridge arr. | | | | 1 10 | | | | 2 2 | | |
| **London** (Euston) dep. | | | | 8SX30 | | | | 8 45 | 10 30 | |
| Bristol (via Birmingham) ,, | | | | | | | | 7 42 | 9ab5 | |
| Birmingham (New Street) ,, | | | | 9SX45 | | | | 11 0 | 11da45 | |
| Bristol (via Severn Tunnel) ,, | | | | | | | | 8SX25 | 5S040 | |
| Cardiff (General) ,, | | | | | | | | 9SX 0 | 6S055 | |
| Hereford ,, | | | | | | | | 10SX27 | 9S015 | |
| Swansea (Victoria) ,, | | | | | | | | 7SX45 | 7 45 | |
| Shrewsbury ,, | | | | | | | | 11SX38 | 11 45 | |
| Crewe ,, | | | | 11 17 | | | | 12gd35 | 1 23 | |
| Stoke-on-Trent ,, | | | | 11SX21 | | | | 11R57 | 12S020 | |
| Stockport ,, | | | | 12 24 | | | | 1 27 | 2 4 | |
| Stalybridge dep. | | | | 1 12 | | | | 2 4 | | 2 20 |
| Mossley | | | | 1 18 | | | | 2 10 | | 2 26 |
| **Oldham** Clegg Street dep. | | | | 1*10 | | | | 2gg0 | | 2D 8 |
| **Oldham** Glodwick Road ,, | | | | 1*12 | | | | 2gg2 | | 2D10 |
| Greenfield dep. | | | 1 20 | 1f29 | | | | 2W20 | | 2 31 |
| Saddleworth | | | 1 24 | 1 33 | | | | | | 2 36 |
| Diggle | | | 1 28 | 1 37 | | | | | | 2 40 |
| Marsden | | 1 35 | 1 36 | 1 46 | | | 2 15 | | | 2 47 |
| Slaithwaite | | 1 40 | 1 43 | 1 54 | | | 2 20 | | | 2 54 |
| Golcar | | 1 44 | 1 47 | 1 58 | | | 2 24 | | | 3 0 |
| Longwood and Milnsbridge | | 1 47 | 1 51 | 2 1 | | | 2 28 | | | 3 3 |
| **Huddersfield** arr. | | 1 54 | 1 58 | 2 8 | | | 2 35 | 2 39 | 2 44 | 3 10 |
| Halifax arr. | | | | 2c46 | | | 3 9 | 3 9 | 3 20 | |
| Bradford (Exchange) ,, | | | | 2 40 | | | 3 39 | 3 39 | 3 56 | |
| **Huddersfield** ¶ dep. | 1 55 | | | 2 15 | | 2 37 | | 2 41 | | 3 22 |
| Bradley | 2 1 | | | 2 21 | | 2 43 | | | | 3 28 |
| Battyeford | 2 5 | | | | | 2 47 | | | | 3 32 |
| Northorpe (Higher) | 2 9 | | | | | 2 51 | | | | 3 36 |
| Heckmondwike (Spen.) ¶ | 2 13 | | | | | 2 55 | | | | 3 40 |
| Liversedge (Spen.) ¶ | 2 16 | | | | | 2 58 | | | | 3 43 |
| Cleckheaton (Spen.) ¶ | 2 20 | | | | | 3 2 | | | | 3 46 |
| Gomersal | 2 25 | | | | | 3 7 | | | | 3 50 |
| Birstall Town | 2 29 | | | | | 3 12 | | | | 3 54 |
| Mirfield | | | | 2 25 | | | | 2 49 | | |
| Wakefield (Kirkgate) arr. | | | | | | | | 3 19 | 3§57 | |
| Normanton ,, | | | | | | | | 3 29 | 4§ 6 | |
| Ravensthorpe & Thornhill dep. | | | | 2 30 | | | | | | |
| Dewsbury (Wellington Road) | | | | 2 34 | | | | 2 55 | | |
| Staincliffe & Batley Carr | | | | 2 38 | | | | | | |
| Batley | | | | 2 41 | | | | 3 0 | | |
| Morley | | | | 2 49 | | | | | | |
| Churwell | | | | | | | | | | |
| Farnley and Wortley | 2 37 | | | 2 55 | | 3 20 | | | | 4 2 |
| **Leeds** (New Station) arr. | 2 45 | | | 3 3 | | 3 28 | | 3 19 | | 4 10 |
| L.&N.E. Hull arr. | | | | | | | | 5 8 | | |
| L.&N.E. York ,, | | | | 4 9 | | 4 36 | | 4 36 | | |
| L.&N.E. Scarborough (Central) ,, | | | | | | | | | | |
| L.&N.E. Harrogate ,, | | | | | | 4b28 | | 4 13 | | 5 3 |
| L.&N.E. Sunderland ,, | | | | | | | | 6 30 | | |
| L.&N.E. Newcastle-on-Tyne ,, | | | | | | 6 29 | | 6 15 | | |

| Station | Express—Liverpool & Manchester to Newcastle. | | | | | | | | | |
|---|---|---|---|---|---|---|---|---|---|---|
| **Liverpool** (Lime Street) dep. | 2 20 | | | | 3 15 | | | | | |
| ,, (Exchange) §§ ,, | | | | | | | | | | |
| Llandudno ,, | 12 5 | | | | 12 40 | | | | | |
| Chester (General) ,, | 1 40 | | | | 2 35 | | | | | |
| Warrington (Bank Quay) ,, | 2 20 | | | | 3 11 | | | | | |
| Blackpool (North) §§ ,, | 12p43 | | | | 1 35 | | | | | |
| ,, (Central) §§ ,, | 12 40 | | | 1q50 | 1M10 | | | | 2 5 | |
| **Manchester** (Exchange) dep. | 3 5 | | 3 15 | 3c30 | 3 58 | | | | 4 12 | |
| Ashton (Charlestown) | | | 3 29 | 3 50 | | | | | 4 25 | |
| Stalybridge arr. | 3 19 | | 3 33 | 3 54 | | | | | 4 29 | |
| **London** (Euston) dep. | | | | | | | | | 11d50 | |
| Bristol (via Birmingham) ,, | | | | | | | | | 10fa35 | |
| Birmingham (New Street) ,, | 12 10 | | | | | | | | 12fa55 | |
| Bristol (via Severn Tunnel) ,, | 10 0 | | | | | | | | | |
| Cardiff (General) ,, | 9 45 | | | | | | | | | |
| Hereford ,, | 11 40 | | | | | | | | | |
| Swansea (Victoria) ,, | | | | | | | | | | |
| Shrewsbury ,, | 12 50 | | | | | | | | 1S010 | |
| Crewe ,, | 1 44 | | | | | | | | 2d38 | |
| Stoke-on-Trent ,, | 1 25 | | | | | | | | | |
| Stockport ,, | 2 45 | | | | | | | | 3d15 | |
| Stalybridge dep. | 3 24 | | 3 34 | 3 55 | | | | | 4 31 | |
| Mossley | | | 3 40 | 4 1 | | | | | 4 37 | |
| **Oldham** Clegg Street dep. | | | 3*27 | | | | | | 4*22 | |
| **Oldham** Glodwick Road ,, | | | 3*29 | | | | | | 4*24 | |
| Greenfield dep. | | | 3 45 | | | | | | 4 42 | |
| Saddleworth | | | 3 50 | | | | | | 4 48 | |
| Diggle | | | 3 54 | | | | | | 4 52 | |
| Marsden | | | 4 2 | | | | | | 5 0 | |
| Slaithwaite | | | 4 9 | | | | | | 5 7 | |
| Golcar | | | 4 13 | | | | | | 5 11 | |
| Longwood and Milnsbridge | | | 4 16 | | | | | | 5 14 | |
| **Huddersfield** arr. | 3 50 | | 4 23 | | 4 35 | | | | 5 22 | |
| Halifax arr. | 4 23 | | | | 5 35 | | | | 5m58 | |
| Bradford (Exchange) ,, | 4 50 | | | | 5 16 | | | | 6a15 | |
| **Huddersfield** ¶ dep. | 3 55 | 4 5 | | | 4 39 | 4 50 | 5 6 | 5 18 | | |
| Bradley | | 4 11 | | | | 4 56 | 5 12 | 5 24 | | |
| Battyeford | | | | | | | 5 16 | | | |
| Northorpe (Higher) | | | | | | | 5 20 | | | |
| Heckmondwike (Spen.) ¶ | | | | | | | 5 24 | | | |
| Liversedge (Spen.) ¶ | | | | | | | 5 27 | | | |
| Cleckheaton (Spen.) ¶ | | | | | | | 5 30 | | | |
| Gomersal | | | | | | | 5 34 | | | |
| Birstall Town | | | | | | | 5 38 | | | |
| Mirfield | | 4 15 | | | | 5 0 | | 5 28 | | |
| Wakefield (Kirkgate) arr. | | 4 59 | 4 59 | | | | | 5 58 | | |
| Normanton ,, | | 5 20 | 5 20 | | | | | 6 7 | | |
| Ravensthorpe & Thornhill dep. | | 4 21 | | | | 5 6 | | 5 33 | | |
| Dewsbury (Wellington Road) | | 4 25 | | | | 5f15 | | 5 37 | | |
| Staincliffe & Batley Carr | | | | | | 5 18 | | 5 41 | | |
| Batley | | 4 30 | | | | 5 21 | | 5 44 | | |
| Morley | | 4 40 | | | | 5 29 | | 5 52 | | |
| Churwell | | 4 41 | | | | 5 33 | | 5 57 | | |
| Farnley and Wortley | | 4 47 | | | | 5 36 | 5 46 | 6 0 | | |
| **Leeds** (New Station) arr. | 4 24 | 4 55 | | | 5 8 | 5 43 | 5 53 | 6 9 | | |
| L.&N.E. Hull arr. | | 6 26 | | | | | | | | |
| L.&N.E. York ,, | 5 12 | | | | 6 0 | 6 39 | | | | |
| L.&N.E. Scarborough (Central) ,, | 6 10 | | | | 7 15 | | | | | |
| L.&N.E. Harrogate ,, | 5 13 | | | | 5u55 | | 6 34 | | | |
| L.&N.E. Sunderland ,, | 7 0 | | | | 8 20 | | | | | |
| L.&N.E. Newcastle-on-Tyne ,, | 7 24 | | | | 8 8 | | | | | |

| Station | Through Express (with Buffet Car)—Liverpool and Manchester to Hull. | | Saturdays excepted. | Saturdays excepted. | Saturdays excepted. | Saturdays only. | Through Train from Stockport. | Thursdays and Fridays only. | Restaurant Car Express—Liverpool to Newcastle (Saturdays excepted), Manchester to Newcastle (Saturdays only). | |
|---|---|---|---|---|---|---|---|---|---|---|
| **Liverpool** (Lime Street) dep. | 4 0 | | | | | | | | 5SX0 | |
| ,, (Exchange) §§ ,, | | | | | | | | | 4S035 | |
| Llandudno ,, | 1 45 | | | | | | | | 2 35 | |
| Chester (General) ,, | 3 22 | | | | | | | | 4 13 | 3 22 |
| Warrington (Bank Quay) ,, | 3 50 | | | | | | | | 4 45 | 4 25 |
| Blackpool (North) §§ ,, | 2 50 | | | | | | | | | |
| ,, (Central) §§ ,, | | | | | | | | | 3 10 | 2q 8 |
| **Manchester** (Exchange) dep. | 4 47 | | | | | | 5V 3 | 5C40 | 5 53 | 5 27 |
| Ashton (Charlestown) | | | | | | | 5V23 | 6 0 | | 5 47 |
| Stalybridge arr. | 5 2 | | | | | | 5V29 | 6 4 | | 5 51 |
| **London** (Euston) dep. | | | | | | | 12dc5 | | | 12dg 5 |
| Bristol (via Birmingham) ,, | 10 35 | | | | | | 12 35 | | | 12SX35 |
| Birmingham (New Street) ,, | 2 0 | | | | | | 2 52 | | | 2SX52 |
| Bristol (via Severn Tunnel) ,, | | | | | | | 12 20 | | | 12SX20 |
| Cardiff (General) ,, | | | | | | | 12 35 | | | 12SX35 |
| Hereford ,, | | | | | | | 2 14 | | | 2SX14 |
| Swansea (Victoria) ,, | | | | | | | 10 25 | | | 10SX25 |
| Shrewsbury ,, | | | | | | | 3 27 | | | 3SX27 |
| Crewe ,, | 3 32 | | | | | | 4 25 | | | 4SX25 |
| Stoke-on-Trent ,, | 3 15 | | | | | | | | | |
| Stockport ,, | 4 30 | | | | | | 5 21 | | | 5SX21 |
| Stalybridge dep. | 5 5 | | | 5 12 | | | 5 42 | 6 5 | | 5 54 |
| Mossley | | | | 5 18 | | | | 6 10 | | 5 59 |
| **Oldham** Clegg Street dep. | 4*52 | | | | | | | Stop | | 5 47 |
| **Oldham** Glodwick Road ,, | 4*54 | | | | | | | | | 5 49 |
| Greenfield dep. | 5f20 | | | 5 23 | | | | | | 6 5 |
| Saddleworth | | | | Stop | | | | | | 6 11 |
| Diggle | | | | | | | | | | 6 15 |
| Marsden | | | 5 20 | | | 5 38 | | 5 57 | | 6 23 |
| Slaithwaite | | | 5 26 | | | 5 43 | | 6 2 | | 6 30 |
| Golcar | | | 5 30 | | | 5 47 | | 6 6 | | 6 34 |
| Longwood and Milnsbridge | | | 5 34 | | | 5 50 | | 6 9 | | 6 38 |
| **Huddersfield** arr. | 5 40 | | 5 43 | | | 5 58 | 6 9 | 6 16 | 6 33 | 6 47 |
| Halifax arr. | 6 31 | | 6 31 | | | 6 31 | 7 8 | 7 8 | | |
| Bradford (Exchange) ,, | 6 59 | | 6 59 | | | 6 59 | 7 17 | 7ba17 | 7S07 | 7SX20 |
| **Huddersfield** ¶ dep. | 5 43 | | | 5 47 | 6 7 | 6 7 | | | 6 36 | 6 55 |
| Bradley | | | | 5 53 | 6 13 | 6 13 | | | | 7 1 |
| Battyeford | | | | | 6 17 | 6 17 | | | | |
| Northorpe (Higher) | | | | | 6 21 | 6 21 | | | | |
| Heckmondwike (Spen.) ¶ | | | | | 6 25 | 6 25 | | | | |
| Liversedge (Spen.) ¶ | | | | | 6 28 | 6 28 | | | | |
| Cleckheaton (Spen.) ¶ | | | | | 6 31 | 6 31 | | | | |
| Gomersal | | | | | 6 35 | 6 35 | | | | |
| Birstall Town | | | | | 6 39 | 6 39 | | | | |
| Mirfield | | | | 5 57 | | | | | | 7 5 |
| Wakefield (Kirkgate) arr. | | | | 6 50 | | 6§50 | | | | 7 54 |
| Normanton ,, | | | | 6 59 | | 6§59 | | | | 8 6 |
| Ravensthorpe & Thornhill dep. | | | | 6 3 | | | | | | 7 11 |
| Dewsbury (Wellington Road) | 5 55 | | | 6 7 | | | | | | 7 15 |
| Staincliffe & Batley Carr | | | | 6 11 | | | | | | 7 19 |
| Batley | 6W4 | | | 6 14 | | | | | | 7 22 |
| Morley | 6 12 | | | 6 22 | | | | | | 7 30 |
| Churwell | | | | 6 26 | | | | | | 7 35 |
| Farnley and Wortley | | | | 6 29 | 6 48 | 6 48 | | | | 7 38 |
| **Leeds** (New Station) arr. | 6 21 | | | 6 37 | 6 55 | 6 56 | | | 7 5 | 7 46 |
| L.&N.E. Hull arr. | 7 45 | | | 8 37 | | | | | | |
| L.&N.E. York ,, | 7 11 | | | | | | | | 7 55 | |
| L.&N.E. Scarborough (Central) ,, | | | | | | | | | 9 9 | |
| L.&N.E. Harrogate ,, | 7 22 | | | | | | | | 7 41 | |
| L.&N.E. Sunderland ,, | | | | | | | | | 10 18 | |
| L.&N.E. Newcastle-on-Tyne ,, | | | | | | | | | 9 13 | |

| Station | | | Restaurant Car Express—Liverpool to Leeds. | | Saturdays excepted. | | Saturdays only. | Through Train—Stockport to Huddersfield, Halifax and Bradford. |
|---|---|---|---|---|---|---|---|---|
| **Liverpool** (Lime Street) dep. | | | 5 45 | | | | | |
| ,, (Exchange) §§ ,, | | | | | | | | 6 35 |
| Llandudno ,, | | | 3 25 | | | | | 4gb25 |
| Chester (General) ,, | | | 5 13 | | | | | 6X15 |
| Warrington (Bank Quay) ,, | | | 5 46 | | | | | |
| Blackpool (North) §§ ,, | | | 4 25 | | | | | 5 10 |
| ,, (Central) §§ ,, | | | 4 5 | | | | | |
| **Manchester** (Exchange) dep. | 6 5 | | 6 37 | | | 7 0 | | 7V30 |
| Ashton (Charlestown) | 6 19 | | | | | 7 18 | | 7V50 |
| Stalybridge arr. | 6 24 | | 6 51 | | | 7 22 | | 7V54 |
| **London** (Euston) dep. | 12S0 5 | | 1 30 | | | | | 4 10 |
| Bristol (via Birmingham) ,, | 12S035 | | 12 35 | | | | | 2 20 |
| Birmingham (New Street) ,, | 2S052 | | 3 45 | | | | | 5 50 |
| Bristol (via Severn Tunnel) ,, | 12S020 | | | | | | | 2 10 |
| Cardiff (General) ,, | 12S035 | | | | | | | 2 10 |
| Hereford ,, | 2S014 | | | | | | | 4 5 |
| Swansea (Victoria) ,, | 10S025 | | | | | | | 12 50 |
| Shrewsbury ,, | 3S027 | | | | | | | 5 50 |
| Crewe ,, | 4 25 | | 5 13 | | | | | 7 22 |
| Stoke-on-Trent ,, | 4SX27 | | 4S035 | | | | | 7 8 |
| Stockport ,, | 5 43 | | 6 13 | | | | | 8 7 |
| Stalybridge dep. | 6 26 | | 6 56 | | | 7 24 | | 8 24 |
| Mossley | 6 32 | | | | | 7 30 | | |
| **Oldham** Clegg Street dep. | 6bb14 | | | | | 7gg10 | | |
| **Oldham** Glodwick Road ,, | 6bb16 | | | | | 7gg12 | | |
| Greenfield dep. | 6 37 | | | | | 7 35 | | AA |
| Saddleworth | 6 42 | | | | | 7 41 | | |
| Diggle | 6 46 | | | | | 7 45 | | |
| Marsden | 6 53 | | | | 7 35 | 7 52 | | AA |
| Slaithwaite | 7 0 | | | | 7 40 | 7 59 | | AA |
| Golcar | 7 4 | | | | 7 44 | 8 3 | | AA |
| Longwood and Milnsbridge | 7 7 | | | | 7 47 | 8 6 | | AA |
| **Huddersfield** arr. | 7 14 | | 7 21 | | 7 55 | 8 13 | | 8 51 |
| Halifax arr. | | | 8 3 | | | 8 56 | | 9 18 |
| Bradford (Exchange) ,, | | | 8 32 | | | | | 9F47 |
| **Huddersfield** ¶ dep. | 7 20 | | 7 24 | 7 35 | | 8 15 | | |
| Bradley | 7 26 | | | 7 41 | | 8 21 | | |
| Battyeford | 7 30 | | | | | | | |
| Northorpe (Higher) | 7 34 | | | | | | | |
| Heckmondwike (Spen.) ¶ | 7 38 | | | | | | | |
| Liversedge (Spen.) ¶ | 7 41 | | | | | | | |
| Cleckheaton (Spen.) ¶ | 7 44 | | | | | | | |
| Gomersal | 7 48 | | | | | | | |
| Birstall Town | 7 52 | | | | | | | |
| Mirfield | | | | 7 45 | | 8 25 | | |
| Wakefield (Kirkgate) arr. | | | | | | 9 15 | | 9 58 |
| Normanton ,, | | | | | | 9 26 | | 10 8 |
| Ravensthorpe & Thornhill dep. | | | | 7 50 | | 8 31 | | |
| Dewsbury (Wellington Road) | | | | 7 54 | | 8 35 | 9 5 | |
| Staincliffe & Batley Carr | | | | | | | | |
| Batley | | | | 8 0 | | 8 41 | 9 9 | |
| Morley | | | | 8 10 | | 8 49 | 9 17 | |
| Churwell | | | | | | 8 53 | | |
| Farnley and Wortley | 8 0 | | | 8 16 | | 8 56 | 9 24 | |
| **Leeds** (New Station) arr. | 8 9 | | 7 51 | 8 24 | | 9 3 | 9 31 | |
| L.&N.E. Hull arr. | 9S025 | | 10ae5 | | | | 12 3 | |
| L.&N.E. York ,, | | | 8 56 | 9 10 | | 10 10 | 11 25 | |
| L.&N.E. Scarborough (Central) ,, | | | 10S015 | | | | | |
| L.&N.E. Harrogate ,, | | | 9U12 | 9 12 | | 9 59 | 10b20 | |
| L.&N.E. Sunderland ,, | | | | 11 12 | | | 6 12 | |
| L.&N.E. Newcastle-on-Tyne ,, | | | | 10 55 | | | 5 0 | |

For Notes, see page 198.

A thin line between the hour and minute figures indicates p.m.

# LIVERPOOL, MANCHESTER (EXCHANGE), STALYBRIDGE, HUDDERSFIELD, LEEDS (NEW), YORK, HULL, AND NEWCASTLE-ON-TYNE.

## WEEK DAYS—continued.

| | | | Buffet Car—Liverpool (L. St.) to Leeds (New) | Saturdays excepted. | | | Express—Stockport to Huddersfield and Halifax. | Saturdays excepted. | Saturdays only. | Saturdays only. | | Saturdays excepted. | Saturdays only. | | Through Train—Crewe to Leeds. |
|---|---|---|---|---|---|---|---|---|---|---|---|---|---|---|---|
| **Liverpool** (Lime Street) ...dep. | | | 7 0 | | | | | | | | 8 40 | | | 10 40 | |
| ,, (Exchange) §§ ... ,, | | | | | | 7 18 | | | | | 8 40 | | 9 5 | | |
| Llandudno ,, | | | | | | 5 40 | | | | | | | 7pp30 | | 9X10 |
| Chester (General) ,, | | | 6 35 | | | 7 15 | | | | | | | 9pp15 | | 11X 5 |
| Warrington (Bank Quay) ,, | | | 7 23 | | | 7 45 | | | | | 8 55 | | 9pp55 | 11 55 | |
| Blackpool (North) §§ ,, | | | 5K30 | | | | | | | | 7 50 | | 8 40 | | |
| ,, (Central) §§ ,, | | | 5B27 | | | 6 30 | | | | | 7k35 | | 8 10 | | 9X45 |
| **Manchester** (Exchange) ...dep. | | | 8 20 | | | 9 15 | | | | | 10 10 | | 11C 6 | 12H 0 | |
| Ashton (Charlestown) | | | 8 33 | | | 9 29 | | | | | 10 23 | | 11 24 | | |
| Stalybridge ... arr. | | | 8 40 | | | 9 33 | | | | | 10 29 | | 11 28 | | |
| **London** (Euston) ...dep. | | | | | | | 6n10 | | | | | | | 6p10 | 8 45 |
| Bristol (via Birmingham) ,, | | | | | | | | | | | | | | 5SO0 | 7 20 |
| Birmingham (New Street) ,, | | | | | | | 6 42 | | | | | | | 8SO20 | 10 15 |
| Bristol (via Severn Tunnel) ,, | | | | | | 4SO13 | 4 13 | | | | | | | | 7 20 |
| Cardiff (General) ,, | | | | | | 4SO25 | 4 25 | | | | | | | | 7 25 |
| Hereford ,, | | | | | | 6SO 5 | 6 5 | | | | | | | | 9 15 |
| Swansea (Victoria) ,, | | | | | | 2SO45 | 2 45 | | | | | | | | 6 45 |
| Shrewsbury ,, | | | | | | 7SO18 | 7 18 | | | | | | | 8 5 | 10 40 |
| Crewe ,, | | | | | | 8SO 7 | 9n8 | | | | | | | 9p45 | 12 30 |
| Stoke-on-Trent ,, | | | | | | 7SO13 | 7n9 | | | | 8 37 | t | | 9p35 | |
| Stockport ,, | | | | | | 8SO50 | 9n44 | | | | 10 0 | | | 12 35 | |
| Stalybridge ...dep. | | | 8 42 | | | 9 35 | | | | | 10 34 | | 11 30 | | |
| Mossley | | | 8 48 | | | 9 41 | A | | | | 10 40 | | 11 36 | | |
| **Oldham** (Clegg Street ...dep. | | | 8dd30 | | | 9*20 | | | 9 43 | | 10*28 | | 11*25 | | |
| **Oldham** (Glodwick Road ,, | | | 8dd32 | | | 9*22 | | | 9 45 | | 10*30 | | 11*27 | | |
| Greenfield | | | 8 53 | | | 9g49 | A | | 9 57 | | 10 45 | | 11 43 | | |
| Saddleworth | | | 9 0 | | | | | | 10 2 | | 10 51 | | 11 48 | | |
| Diggle | | | 9 4 | | | | | | 10 6 | | 10 55 | | 11 52 | | |
| Marsden | | 8 58 | 9 11 | | | | A | | 10 12 | 10 30 | 11 2 | 11 15 | 11 58 | | |
| Slaithwaite | | 9 3 | 9 19 | | | | A | | 10 18 | 10 35 | 11 8 | 11 20 | | | |
| Golcar | | 9 7 | 9 23 | | | | A | | 10 22 | 10 39 | 11 12 | 11 24 | | | |
| Longwood and Milnsbridge | | 9 10 | 9 26 | | | | A | | 10 25 | 10 42 | 11 15 | 11 27 | | | |
| **Huddersfield** ... arr. | | 9 16 | 9 34 | | | 10 9 | 10e26 | | 10 33 | 10 51 | 11 23 | 11 34 | | 1Q20 | 1 51 |
| Halifax ... arr. | | | 10 26 | | | | 10e51 | | | 11 26 | | | | | 6Ga47 |
| Bradford (Exchange) ,, | | | 10 18 | | | | 11 19 | | 11 19 | | | | | | 6Ga3[illegible] |
| **Huddersfield** ¶ ...dep. | 9 0 | 9SO40 | 9 45 | 9 56 | | 10 14 | | 10 32 | 10 48 | | 11 28 | | | | 2 5 |
| Bradley | 9 6 | 9SO46 | 9 51 | 10 2 | | | | 10 38 | 10 55 | | | | | | |
| Battyeford | 9 10 | 9SO50 | | 10 6 | | | | 10 42 | 10 59 | | | | | | |
| Northorpe (Higher) | 9 14 | | | 10 10 | | | | 10 46 | 11 3 | | | | | | |
| Heckmondwike (Spen.) ¶ | 9 18 | | | 10 14 | | | | 10 50 | 11 7 | | | | | | |
| Liversedge (Spen.) ¶ | 9 21 | | | 10 17 | | | | 10 53 | 11 10 | | | | | | |
| Cleckheaton (Spen.) ¶ | 9 24 | | | 10 20 | | | | 10 58 | 11 13 | | | | | | |
| Gomersal | 9 28 | | | 10 24 | | | | 11 2 | 11 17 | | | | | | |
| Birstall Town | 9 32 | | | | | | | | 11 21 | | | | | | |
| Mirfield | | | 9W59 | | | 10 22 | | | | | 11g40 | | | | |
| Wakefield (Kirkgate) ... arr. | | | | | | 10 47 | | | | | | | | | |
| Normanton ,, | | | | | | 10 56 | | | | | | | | | |
| Ravensthorpe & Thornhill ...dep. | | | 10 4 | | | | | | | | 11SO45 | | | | |
| Dewsbury (Wellington Road) | | | 10 8 | | | 10 28 | | | | | 11 47 | | | | |
| Staincliffe & Batley Carr | | | | | | | | | | | | | | | |
| Batley | | | 10 12 | | | 10 34 | | | | | 11 52 | | | | |
| Morley | | | 10 22 | | | | | | | | 12 2 | | | | |
| Churwell | | | | | | | | | | | | | | | |
| Farnley & Wortley | 9 40 | | 10 28 | 10 34 | | | | | | | | | | | |
| **Leeds** (New Station) ...arr. | 9 47 | | 10 42 | 10 41 | | 10 54 | | 11 18 | 11 38 | | 12 15 | | | | 2 38 |
| L.&N.E.R. Hull ... arr. | 12 3 | | | | | | | | | | | | | | 4‖35 |
| York ,, | 11SX10 | | 11SO20 | | | | | | | | 2j55 | | | | 3 22 |
| Scarborough (Central) ,, | | | | | | | | | | | | | | | 5‖55 |
| Harrogate ,, | | | | | | 11 42 | | | | | | | | | 4‖38 |
| Sunderland ,, | 6j12 | | 6ja12 | | | | | | | | | | | | 6 12 |
| Newcastle-on-Tyne ,, | 1j6 | | 8ja[illegible] | | | | | | | | 5j10 | | | | 6 0 |

## SUNDAYS.

| | | Through Train—Stockport to Halifax and Bradford. | | | Through Express Train—Liverpool and Manchester to Newcastle. | Express—London (Euston) to Halifax and Bradford. | | | | | | Monday mornings. | Monday mornings. Through Train—Crewe to Leeds. |
|---|---|---|---|---|---|---|---|---|---|---|---|---|---|
| **Liverpool** (Lime Street) ...dep. | | | 7 35 | 10 5 | 11 40 | | 2 55 | | | 6 35 | 8 0 | 10 35 | |
| ,, (Exchange) §§ ... ,, | | | 8 0 | | | | | | | | | | |
| Llandudno ,, | 10X50 | | | | 9 45 | 12X50 | | | | | 6 10 | | 9X 5 |
| Chester (General) ,, | 2X 0 | | 7 5 | | 11 7 | 3X 3 | 3 10 | | | | 7 40 | | 11X 0 |
| Warrington (Bank Quay) ,, | | | 7 57 | 8 45 | 11 50 | | 3 41 | | | 6 0 | | 11 55 | |
| Blackpool (North) §§ ,, | | | 7 10 | | | | | | | 5 10 | 7ca0 | 8 55 | |
| ,, (Central) §§ ,, | | | 6 58 | 8 0 | | | 2 25 | | | 5B20 | 7 0 | 9 0 | 9r25 |
| **Manchester** (Exchange) ...dep. | 7 50 | | 10 20 | 11 5 | 12 45 | | 5 8 | | | 8 40 | 9 6 | 12H0 | |
| Ashton (Charlestown) | 8 5 | | 10 37 | 11 20 | 12 59 | | 5 21 | | | 8 54 | 9 22 | | |
| Stalybridge ... arr. | 8 10 | | 10 41 | 11 24 | 1 3 | | 5 26 | | | 8 58 | 9 26 | | |
| **London** (Euston) ...dep. | 12 40 | | | | | 12 35 | | | | | | | 7 30 |
| Bristol (via Birmingham) ,, | 8Z 0 | | | | | 9 35 | | | | 2 0 | | | 7 20 |
| Birmingham (New Street) ,, | 3 1 | | | | | 2 0 | | | | 4 40 | | | 10 15 |
| Bristol (via Severn Tunnel) ,, | 11Z50 | | | | | | | | | 12 35 | | | 5 50 |
| Cardiff (General) ,, | 12 5 | | | | | | | | | 12 55 | | | 6 15 |
| Hereford ,, | 1 50 | | | | | 7 15 | | | | 2bd35 | | | 8 0 |
| Swansea (Victoria) ,, | | | | | | 9 45 | | | | | | | |
| Shrewsbury ,, | 3 15 | | | | | 12 25 | | | | 3bd52 | | | 9 45 |
| Crewe ,, | 5 5 | 8 37 | | | | 4 5 | | | | 4bd42 | | | 12 30 |
| Stoke-on-Trent ,, | | 8 15 | | | 10 10 | 2 30 | | | | 6 25 | | 9 45 | |
| Stockport ,, | 7 35 | 10 12 | | | 12 25 | 4 55 | | | | 8 23 | | 12 35 | 1 10 |
| Stalybridge ...dep. | 8 15 | 10 33 | 10 44 | 11 26 | 1 5 | 5 18 | 5 27 | | | 9 0 | 9 36 | | |
| Mossley | 8 21 | | 10 50 | | | | 5 33 | | | 9 6 | | | |
| **Oldham** (Clegg Street ...dep. | | | 10*35 | | 12*40 | | 5*20 | | | 8*50 | | | |
| **Oldham** (Glodwick Road ,, | | | 10*37 | | 12*42 | | 5*22 | | | 8*52 | | | |
| Greenfield | 8 26 | | 10g58 | | 1 14 | | 5 37 | | | 9 11 | | | |
| Saddleworth | 8 33 | | 11 2 | | | | 5 42 | | | 9 17 | | | |
| Diggle | 8 37 | | 11 6 | | | | 5 46 | | | 9 21 | | | |
| Marsden | 8 44 | | 11 13 | | | | 5 53 | | | 9 28 | | | |
| Slaithwaite | 8 51 | | 11 21 | | | | 5 59 | | | 9 33 | | | |
| Golcar | 8 55 | | 11 26 | | | | 6 3 | | | 9 37 | | | |
| Longwood and Milnsbridge | 8 58 | | 11 29 | | | | 6 6 | | | 9 40 | | | |
| **Huddersfield** ... arr. | 9 3 | 11 0 | 11 34 | 11 54 | 1 36 | 5 46 | 6 11 | | | 9 47 | 10 0 | 1 20 | 1 55 |
| Halifax ... arr. | 9 55 | 11 32 | | | 3 27 | 6 18 | 7 13 | | | | 10 41 | | 5 47 |
| Bradford (Exchange) ,, | 10 40 | 12 0 | | 1 19 | 4 5 | 6 40 | 7 10 | | | | 10 56 | | 6 32 |
| **Huddersfield** ¶ ...dep. | 9 8 | | 11 40 | 11 57 | 1 41 | | | 6 35 | 8 20 | 9 51 | 10 10 | | 2 5 |
| Bradley | | | | | | | | | | | | | |
| Battyeford | | | | | | | | | | | | | |
| Northorpe (Higher) | | | | | | | | | | | | | |
| Heckmondwike (Spen.) ¶ | | | | | | | | | | | | | |
| Liversedge (Spen.) ¶ | | | | | | | | | | | | | |
| Cleckheaton (Spen.) ¶ | | | | | | | | | | | | | |
| Gomersal | | | | | | | | | | | | | |
| Birstall Town | | | | | | | | | | | | | |
| Mirfield | 9 17 | | 11f54 | | 1 50 | | | 6 45 | 8 29 | 10 0 | 10 19 | | |
| Wakefield (Kirkgate) ... arr. | 10 40 | | | 12 52 | 3 55 | | | | 9 56 | | | | 6 47 |
| Normanton ,, | 10 50 | | | 1 1 | 4 5 | | | | 10 5 | | | | 6 57 |
| Ravensthorpe & Thornhill ...dep. | 9 23 | | 11 58 | | | | | 6 50 | 8 34 | | | | |
| Dewsbury (Wellington Road) | 9 27 | | 12W5 | 12f16 | 1 57 | | | 6 54 | 8 38 | 10 7 | 10W30 | | |
| Staincliffe & Batley Carr | | | | | | | | | | | | | |
| Batley | 9 34 | | 12 10 | 12 21 | 2 2 | | | 7 0 | 8 44 | | 10 35 | | |
| Morley | 9 42 | | 12 18 | 12 29 | | | | 7 8 | 8 52 | | 10 43 | | |
| Churwell | | | | | | | | | | | | | |
| Farnley & Wortley | | | | | | | | | | | | | |
| **Leeds** (New Station) ...arr. | 10 1 | | 12 30 | 12 39 | 2 22 | | | 7 21 | 9 5 | 10 31 | 10 52 | | 2 38 |
| L.&N.E.R. Hull ... arr. | | | | 2 0 | 5 5 | | | | | | | | 4 35 |
| York ,, | | | | | 3 28 | | | 9 38 | 11 4 | | 2 55 | | 3 23 |
| Scarborough (Central) ,, | | | | | 6 55 | | | | | | | | 5 55 |
| Harrogate ,, | | | | 2cb30 | 5 12 | | | 8b15 | 10b25 | | | | 4 38 |
| Sunderland ,, | | | | | 5 54 | | | 10b51 | 5 29 | | | | 6 53 |
| Newcastle-on-Tyne ,, | | | | | 5 25 | | | 10b[illegible] | 1 6 | | 5 10 | | 6 0 |

¶ For other trains between **Huddersfield, Heckmondwike (Cen.), Liversedge (Cen.), and Cleckheaton (Cen.),** see page 297.

*—One class only.
††—Pullman Car Express from Leeds (Central), extra charge.
‡—Via Huddersfield & Brighouse.
§§—Via Manchester. Passengers change from Victoria to Exchange stations at Manchester.
‖—On Sundays arrives Hull 4.24, Scarboro' 4.40, Harrogate 8.2 a.m.
**A**—Calls when required to set down from London on notice being given to the guard at Stockport.
**a**—On Saturdays arrives Bradford (Exch.) 6.25 p.m. Passengers from London (Euston), Birmingham, Crewe and Stockport cross from Manchester (London Rd.) to (Victoria) Station at their own expense and arrive Bradford (Exchange) 5.49 p.m. daily.
**AA**—Calls when required to set down from stations South of Crewe on notice being given to the guard at Stockport.
**ab**—Will not apply on Thursday, March 25th, 1937.
**ae**—On Saturdays arrives Hull 9.25 p.m.
**B**—Via Manchester (Exchange). **b**—Via Leeds (Central).
**ba**—On Saturdays arrives Bradford 7.7 p.m.
**bb**—On Saturdays leaves Oldham (Clegg St.) 6.20 and Glodwick Road 6.22 p.m.
**bd**—Runs 10 minutes later, November 15th, 1936, to March 21st inclusive, 1937.
**C**—Departs Manchester (Victoria).
**c**—Passengers from London (Euston), Stoke and Stockport only, and cross Manchester from (London Rd.) to (Victoria) Station at their own expense.
**ca**—Commences October 25th, 1936.
**cb**—By Pullman Car Express from Leeds (Central). Extra charge. This time will not apply on December 25th, 1936, and March 26th and 28th, 1937.
**D**—Saturdays only. One class only.
**d**—Via Oldham and Greenfield. No connection to Mossley.
**da**—On Thursday, March 25th, 1937, leaves Birmingham 11.40 a.m.
**dc**—On Thursday, December 24th, 1936, and Thursday, March 25th, 1937, leaves London (Euston) 1.22 p.m.
**dd**—One class only except on Sats. On Sats. leaves Oldham (Clegg Street) 8.35 and Glodwick Road 8.37 p.m.
**dg**—Saturdays excepted. On Thursdays, December 24th, 1936, and March 25th, 1937, leaves London (Euston) 1.22 p.m.
**E**—Applies to passengers from London (Euston), Crewe and Stockport arriving and departing Manchester (Victoria). Depart from Crewe 6.45 and Stockport 7.58 a.m.
**e**—Arrives Huddersfield 10.22 and Halifax at 10.47 p.m. on Saturdays. On December 24th, 1936, arrives 7 minutes later.
**F**—Arrives at 10.1 p.m. on Saturdays. Passengers can arrive 9.57 p.m. on Saturdays by changing at Huddersfield.
**FO**—Fridays only. **f** Arrives 5 minutes earlier.
**fa**—Applies December 24th, 1936, and March 25th, 1937, only.
**G**—Leaves Birmingham (New St.) 2.30 a.m. on Mondays.
**g**—Arrives 3 minutes earlier.
**gb**—Via Crewe. On Saturdays leaves Llandudno 4.50 p.m.
**gd**—On Saturdays leaves Crewe 12.25 p.m.
**gg**—One class only except on Saturdays.
**H**—Manchester (London Road Station).
**h**—Passengers can arrive Harrogate at 2.43 p.m. via Leeds (Central)
**J**—On Saturdays arrives Harrogate 12.59 p.m.
**j**—Sunday mornings excepted.
**ja**—Sunday mornings only.
**K**—Saturdays excepted and arrives Manchester (Exchange)
**k**—On Saturdays leaves Blackpool (Central) at 8.0 p.m.
**MO**—Mondays only.
**M**—Saturdays excepted. On Saturdays to October 17th inclusive, 1936, departs Blackpool (Central) 1.50 p.m.
**m**—Passengers from London (Euston), Birmingham, Crewe and Stockport cross from Manchester (London Road) to (Victoria) Station at their own expense and arrive Halifax 5.26 p.m.
**N**—Leaves Llandudno 10.50 a.m., Chester 12.24 and Warrington 12.57 p.m. on Saturdays.
**n**—Leaves Warrington 9.38 a.m., Chester 9.0 a.m., London (Euston) 6.0, Crewe 8.45 p.m., Stoke-on-Trent 7.13 and Stockport 9.40 p.m. on Saturdays. On December 24th, 1936, leaves Crewe 9.15 and Stockport 9.51 p.m.
**P**—On Saturdays departs Blackpool (North) 12.30 p.m.
**p**—Leaves London (Eust.) 6.40, Crewe 10.17, Stoke-on-Trent 10.10 p.m. on Saturdays.
**pp**—Passengers change from Exchange to Victoria Station at Manchester.
**Q**—Arrives Huddersfield 7.33 a.m. on Sundays.
**q**—Applies on Saturdays to October 17th, 1936.
**R**—Applies Thursdays and Saturdays only.
**r**—Via Crewe. Commencing October 25th, 1936, departs Blackpool (Central) 9.50 p.m.
**SO**—Saturdays only. **SX**—Saturdays excepted.
**T**—Passengers can arrive 4.37 p.m. by Pullman Car Express from Darlington, extra charge.
**t**—On Saturdays leaves Blackpool (North) 8.17 a.m.
**U**—Passengers can arrive Harrogate 8.45 p.m. by Pullman Car Express from Leeds (Cen.). Extra charge.
**u**—On Saturdays arrives Harrogate 6.22 p.m.
**V**—Leaves Victoria Station, Manchester. Passengers change at Stalybridge for stations beyond. **W**—Arrives 4 minutes earlier.
**X**—Via Crewe. **Y**—Warrington (Arpley).
**y**—On Saturdays departs Blackpool (Central) 7.28 a.m.
**Z**—Saturday night.

When the National Benzole Association was officially inaugurated in March 1919, it was decided that it should become its own distributor of the petroleum spirit, so locations were chosen that could easily be served by rail with bulk deliveries. During the early 1920s the LMS provided a siding to the terminal which was an extension of the Heckmondwike Spen goods yard. The National Benzole Company transferred its operation to Leeds in the early 1960s, but the owners of the chemical plant upgraded the siding for their own use, until it was dismantled around 1970.

In the early 1920s motor buses were starting to capture short distance trade from the railways. In view of the poor service being offered between Huddersfield and Leeds (via the Spen Valley) it is little wonder that bus companies seized the opportunity to take this trade away from the railway.

By 1928, G.H. Kilburn & Sons who operated the "Ideal Bus Company" from a depot at Heckmondwike, were offering a half-hourly service throughout the day between Huddersfield and Leeds. Local omnibus companies were beginning to combine their resources and form themselves into larger organizations. G.H. Kilburn & Sons were merged with the "Yorkshire Company" in 1929, and this later became the "Yorkshire Woollen District Transport Company" in 1935.

1935 was the Silver Jubilee year of King George V and to celebrate this, on Monday 6th May the LMS offered cheap return tickets at single fare prices, both first and third class, by any train to any station within a radius of 60 miles.

To coincide with the start of the summer timetable on 8th July the station known as Upper Birstal was renamed Birstall Town. The LMS probably wanted to give the station a more central image, as the original LNWR station named Birstal, at the terminus of the short branch from Batley by the crossroads of the A62 and A652 had closed to passengers on 31st December, 1916. Secondly the LMS may have wished to conform with the practice of spelling the word Birstall with two "l"s.

Like many place names Birstall has had various spellings over the centuries, the earliest recorded reference (dated 1202) using the spelling *BURSTALL*. In 1296 the Wakefield Court Rolls refer to it as *BIRSTALL*, this has alternated with *BIRSTAL* and occasionally other variations over the centuries.

It is sometimes believed that the LNWR was wrong in using the spelling *BIRSTAL* but this is not so. The Birstal Board of Health (later U.D.C.) used the spelling *BIRSTAL* on its official documents so the LNWR, receiving documents from the Board would naturally spell the word likewise.

The LNWR provided stables at all the goods yards except Northorpe to care for the well-being of the horses owned by the company. By 1938 the LMS must have ceased using the stables building at Liversedge Spen, because it was "let" and converted by W.A. Crockford for use as a wholesale fish merchant's business. This company stayed at Liversedge Spen together with Rawdon Allott, the coal merchant, until 1967.

The LMS offered a substantial holiday trips programme until the outbreak of World War II in 1939. An early start (before 6.00 am) was required for a

## THE EARLY YEARS

trip to Windsor, whereas a trip to Southport departed as late as 5.00 pm. Another interesting point is that the monthly return tickets were valid with unlimited breaks of journey, both outward and return.

The war brought a severe curtailment of passenger services, which had steadily built up during the 1920s and 1930s era and so provided a fairly decent service. Throughout the war and afterwards this meagre service remained until the stations were finally closed in the 1950s.

A skilful blend of the old and the new. This ventilator shaft to Gildersome tunnel stands unobtrusive amidst its more modern surroundings on Gildersome Spur industrial estate. *Author*

# CHEAP LMS TRIPS 1938

## INCLUDING
# LIVERSEDGE, CLECKHEATON and HECKMONDWIKE HOLIDAYS

EVERY DAY, Sunday to Saturday, Aug. 28th to Sept. 3rd. CHEAP DAY RETURN TICKETS from Liversedge, Cleckheaton and Heckmondwike to ANY L.M.S. STATION within a RADIUS OF 60 MILES. Available by Any Train on the day of issue.

### MONTHLY RETURN TICKETS
AT APPROXIMATELY

1D. A MILE — 3rd CLASS
1½D. A MILE — 1st CLASS

ANY DAY — ANY TRAIN
TO ANY STATION IN ENGLAND, WALES and SCOTLAND.

Valid for a Calendar Month with Unlimited breaks of journey outward or return.

Also Cheap Holiday Tickets to Ireland, Isle of Man, Channel Islands, etc.

SCARBOROUGH ...... 4/9
Thursday, Sept. 1st.
BATTYEFORD ............ dep. 11.35 a.m.
NORTHORPE (Higher) ... ,, 11.40 a.m.
HECKMONDWIKE (Sp.) ... ,, 11.45 a.m.
LIVERSEDGE (Spen) ... ,, 11.50 a.m.
CLECKHEATON (Spen) ... ,, 11.55 a.m.
GOMERSAL ............ ,, 12.0 noon
BIRSTALL TOWN ...... ,, 12.5 p.m.
Scarborough arr. 2.15. Return 10.20 p.m.

LONGSIGHT ... ... 1/7
(for Belle Vue)
Reduced Admission Tickets to Belle Vue Gardens, 6d. Adults, 3d. Children to be obtained at the Booking Office.
Saturday, August 27th.
BIRSTALL TOWN ...... dep. 5.50 p.m.
GOMERSAL ............ ,, 5.55 p.m.
CLECKHEATON (Spen) ... ,, 6. 0 p.m.
LIVERSEDGE (Spen) ... ,, 6. 5 p.m.
HECKMONDWIKE (Spen) ... ,, 6.10 p.m.
NORTHORPE (Higher) ... ,, 6.15 p.m.
BATTYEFORD ............ ,, 6.20 p.m.
Return: Longsight 11.25 p.m.

Wednesday, August 31st.
CLECKHEATON (Cen.) ... dep. 6. 5 p.m.
LIVERSEDGE (Cen.) ... ,, 6.10 p.m.
HECKMONDWIKE (Cen.) ... ,, 6.15 p.m.
NORTHORPE (N. Rd.) ... ,, 6.20 p.m.
Return: Longsight 10.35 p.m.

### THE "TIT-BIT" of THE HOLIDAY.
TOWN HOLIDAY WEEKLY TICKETS
AVAILABLE SUNDAY, AUGUST 28th to SATURDAY, SEPTEMBER 3rd inclusive, for UNLIMITED TRAVEL between HECKMONDWIKE, CLECKHEATON, LIVERSEDGE, GOMERSAL and CONISTON, BARROW, FURNESS ABBEY, WINDERMERE (Lake Side), WINDERMERE (Town), MORECAMBE, LANCASTER, PRESTON, BLACKPOOL, FLEETWOOD, SOUTHPORT and MANCHESTER. Also between Ambleside, Bowness, and Lakeside on Windermere Steamers.

COST
FIRST CLASS — 27/9
THIRD CLASS — 18/6

YOU MAY Visit different places each day. Visit the same place each day. Break your journey at Intermediate Stations. Stay overnight if you wish. Travel on to another station without returning home. SEE SPECIAL PAMPHLET.

In addition Holders of these Contracts from Gomersal—Cleckheaton—Liversedge and Heckmondwike may travel free by the Excursion to Rhyl, Colwyn Bay or Llandudno on August 31st. Break of journey is not allowed and passengers must Return same day by the Excursion. Supplementary Tickets (free) must be obtained at Station Booking Offices on or before Tuesday, August 30th.

### Special Inclusive Day Tour to Historic WINDSOR
For Conducted Tour of Castle and the Glorious Thames Valley
Monday, August 29th.
BIRSTALL TOWN ...... dep. 5.38 a.m.
GOMERSAL ............ ,, 5.40 a.m.
CLECKHEATON (Spen) ... ,, 5.48 a.m.
LIVERSEDGE (Spen) ... ,, 5.54 a.m.
HECKMONDWIKE (Spen) ... ,, 5.57 a.m.
NORTHORPE (Higher) ... ,, 6. 0 a.m.
Windsor arr. 12.8 p.m.
INCLUSIVE FARE.—Return Rail, Tour of Windsor Castle, Admission Fees, River Trip, Tea on Steamer.
ADULTS 20/6, CHILDREN 12/-.
Special Train returns Henley 8.0 p.m.
See Bills for full details.
Luncheon out Supper on Return on train 5/6 extra including Gratuities.

### PORT SUNLIGHT ... 4/9
For Special Conducted Tour of Messrs. Lever Bros. Famous Soap Works, with Bookings to
### BIRKENHEAD ...... 4/9
Returning from Liverpool.
Tuesday, August 30th.
BIRSTALL TOWN ...... dep. 11.46 a.m.
GOMERSAL ............ ,, 11.48 a.m.
CLECKHEATON (Spen) ... ,, 11.50 a.m.
LIVERSEDGE (Spen) ... ,, 11.55 a.m.
HECKMONDWIKE (Spen) ... ,, 11.58 a.m.
NORTHORPE (Higher) ... ,, 12. 5 p.m.
Passengers proceed from Port Sunlight to Birkenhead by any train, thence to Liverpool by Ferry (fare 2d.), and return from Liverpool (Lime Street) at 8.20 p.m.

### GLENRIDDING ...... 9/-
FOR LAKE ULLSWATER TOUR
WITH BOOKINGS TO
CLAPHAM 4/2 INGLETON 4/9
KIRKBY LONSDALE 4/9
SEDBERGH 4/9 PENRITH 4/9
Half-Day Trip—Sunday August 28th
HECKMONDWIKE (Sp.) dep. 10.40 a.m.
LIVERSEDGE (Spen) ,, 10.45 a.m.
*CLECKHEATON (Spen) ,, 10.50 a.m.
* Fare to Ingleton 4/2

---

### SPECIALLY REDUCED PERIOD TICKETS
Available Outward Friday, August 26th, to Thursday, September 1st. By any train, to return by any train up to and including Monday, September 5th.
From Cleckheaton, Liversedge, Heckmondwike.

To BLACKPOOL, POULTON, ST. ANNES, THORNTON, ANSDELL, LYTHAM ............ 11/-
To FLEETWOOD ...... 12/1
To *MORECAMBE ...... 12/1

* Tickets to Morecambe available via Leeds only.

RHYL 6/3    COLWYN BAY 6/9
LLANDUDNO 6/9
Wednesday, August 31st
BIRSTALL TOWN ...... dep. 11.25 a.m.
*GOMERSAL ............ ,, 11.30 a.m.
*CLECKHEATON (Spen) ,, 11.35 a.m.
*LIVERSEDGE (Spen) ,, 11.40 a.m.
*HECKMONDWIKE (Sp.) ,, 11.45 a.m.
NORTHORPE (Higher) ,, 11.50 a.m.
BATTYEFORD ............ ,, 11.55 a.m.
Return: Llandudno 9.15, Colwyn Bay 9.30, Rhyl 9.50 p.m.
*Holders of Holiday Contracts may travel free by this excursion to either Rhyl, Colwyn Bay or Llandudno, but must return home the same day by this special train. No break of journey allowed. Supplementary Tickets (free) must be obtained at Station Booking offices on or before Tuesday, August 30th.
Fares shown are from Cleckheaton.

### MORECAMBE ILLUMINATIONS 4/9
MONDAY, August 29th
BATTYEFORD ............ dep. 11.20 a.m.
NORTHORPE (Higher) ... ,, 11.25 a.m.
HECKMONDWIKE (Spen) ,, 11.30 a.m.
LIVERSEDGE (Spen) ... ,, 11.35 a.m.
CLECKHEATON (Spen) ,, 11.40 a.m.
GOMERSAL ............ ,, 11.45 a.m.
BIRSTALL TOWN ...... ,, 11.50 a.m.
Return: Morecambe (Prom) 9.50 p.m.

Saturday, August 27th
HECKMONDWIKE (C.) dep. 1.20 p.m.
LIVERSEDGE (Cen.) ,, 1.25 p.m.
CLECKHEATON (Cen.) ,, 1.30 p.m.
Return: Morecambe (Prom)) 9.50 p.m.

### MORECAMBE ILLUMINATIONS
EVENING TRIPS 2/8
Fare including Admission to Winter Gardens 9d. Extra.

|  | SAT Aug. 27 | SUN. Aug. 28 | TUES. Aug. 30 |
|---|---|---|---|
| Battyeford | 4.50 | 4.0 | 4.15 |
| Northorpe (Higher) | 4.55 | 4.5 | 4.20 |
| Heckmondwike (Sp.) | 5.0 | 4.10 | 4.25 |
| Liversedge (Spen) | 5.5 | 4.15 | 4.28 |
| Cleckheaton (Spen) | 5.8 | 4.20 | 4.30 |
| Gomersal | 5.10 | 4.25 | 4.35 |
| Birstall Town | 5.15 | 4.30 | 4.40 |
| Return: | Midnight p.m. |  |  |
| Morecambe (Prom.) | 12.40 | 10.45 | 10.30 |

Friday, September 2nd
HECKMONDWIKE (C.) dep. 4.30 p.m.
LIVERSEDGE (Cen.) ,, 4.35 p.m.
CLECKHEATON (Cen.) ,, 4.40 p.m.
Return: Morecambe (E. Rd.) 10.30 p.m.

### SOUTHPORT ...... 2/8
Fare, including Admission to Floral Hall 3/8.
Monday, August 29th
BIRSTALL TOWN ...... dep. 1.30 a.m.
GOMERSAL ............ ,, 4.35 p.m.
CLECKHEATON (Spen) ,, 4.40 p.m.
LIVERSEDGE (Spen) ,, 4.45 p.m.
HECKMONDWIKE (Spen) ,, 4.47 p.m.
NORTHORPE (Higher) ,, 4.50 p.m.
BATTYEFORD ............ ,, 4.55 p.m.
Return: Southport 10.50 p.m.

### BLACKPOOL Half Day Trips 4/9
Tuesday, August 30th.
BIRSTALL TOWN ...... dep. 12.25 p.m.
GOMERSAL ............ ,, 12.30 p.m.
CLECKHEATON (Spen) ,, 12.35 p.m.
LIVERSEDGE (Spen) ,, 12.40 p.m.
HECKMONDWIKE (Sp.) ,, 12.45 p.m.
NORTHORPE (Mr.) ,, 12.50 p.m.
BATTYEFORD ............ ,, 12.55 p.m.
Return: Blackpool (North) 9.30 p.m.

---

PLEASE BOOK IN ADVANCE.
TICKETS AND ALL INFORMATION FROM STATIONS AND AGENCIES.
Also full information from H. A. Hocks, District Passenger Manager, 15 17. Lower Briggate, Leeds.

# Chapter Five
## After Nationalization

The railways of Britain were nationalized on 1st January, 1948 although in practice the four groups still operated in their respective regions with a certain amount of rivalry existing. It was, however, different in Yorkshire, where a new North Eastern Region included both ex-LMS and ex-LNER lines.

The only change on the Heaton Lodge and Wortley line as a direct result of nationalization was at Gildersome, where the signal box was renamed Gildersome East, to avoid confusion with the signal box of the same name on the ex-GN line, until then part of the LNER.

When the railway was built it was worked by twelve signal boxes, this had been reduced to nine by 1951. The first box to close was Heckmondwike Station box (about 1920) with the removal of the pointwork and signalling, including the siding which served the bay platform at the station. Cleckheaton No. 1 box was closed and removed together with its pointwork and signalling about 1935, and Cleckheaton No. 2 was renamed Cleckheaton Spen. In 1951 the third signal box closed at Northorpe Higher, which left the spacing of signal boxes along the line as follows:

|  |  |  | m. | yds |
|---|---|---|---|---|
| Spen Valley Junction | to | Battyeford | 1 | 435 |
| Battyeford | to | Heckmondwike Spen | 2 | 1041 |
| Heckmondwike Spen | to | Liversedge Spen | 1 | 199 |
| Liversedge Spen | to | Cleckheaton Spen | 1 | 844 |
| Cleckheaton Spen | to | Gomersal | 1 | 206 |
| Gomersal | to | Birstall Town | 1 | 495 |
| Birstall Town | to | Gildersome East | 2 | 1522 |
| Gildersome East | to | Farnley Junction | 1 | 1306 |

By the beginning of the 1950s the new British Railways Executive had settled down and started to take stock of itself. It was soon realised that the passenger stations on this line were being operated at a considerable loss. The first economy involved the goods yard at Northorpe Higher, which was closed to freight traffic on and from Monday 16th July, 1951, alternative facilities for freight being offered at Mirfield. This did not effect passenger and parcels services from Northorpe Higher station.

The next location to fall victim to rationalization was the passenger station at Birstall Town. An official notice of closure appeared in local newspapers for the week ending 21st July, 1951 which read as follows:

> The passenger train service will be withdrawn from Birstall Town station on and from 1st August, 1951. Bus services are operated by the Yorkshire Woollen District Transport Company between Birstall and the following points, Leeds–Gomersal–Cleckheaton–Huddersfield–Batley–Dewsbury–Bradford, and rail passengers will be booked to and from the most convenient of these stations. Parcels traffic will be dealt with at Batley station at Batley rates plus the appropriate cartage charge where necessary.

The last day of stopping services was Tuesday 31st July, but for several months prior to this, hardly any passengers used the station, the 8.00 am

# THE LEEDS NEW LINE

*[Timetable table: Table 142 — HUDDERSFIELD, HECKMONDWIKE, and LEEDS, showing week days only services between Huddersfield, Battyeford, Northorpe (Higher), Heckmondwike (Spen), Liversedge (Spen), Cleckheaton, Gomersal, and Leeds City; with footnotes about Lockwood departures, Saturday exceptions, and a note: "Where MINUTES under Hours change to a LOWER figure and DARKER type it indicates NEXT HOUR."]*

Passenger timetable for June 1953, which was in force until 20th September just two weeks before the stations closed. The very last timetable was almost identical, the only difference being the withdrawal of the 10.52 (Except Saturdays) Leeds to Huddersfield service.

---

**THE RAILWAY EXECUTIVE**

REGRET TO ANNOUNCE that as the passenger service at CLECKHEATON SPEN STATION is being maintained at a considerable loss it is necessary to WITHDRAW it on and from

**MONDAY, JANUARY 5th, 1953.**

Facilities will be retained for dealing with Special Excursion Trains.

An alternative rail service for passengers to Huddersfield is available at Cleckheaton Central. An alternative service providing three buses to the hour is operated by the Yorkshire Woollen District Transport Co. for passengers to Leeds from a stop about 200 yards from the station.

Parcels traffic will be concentrated at Cleckheaton Central Station and livestock in vehicles will be dealt with at Liversedge Station.

Any trader or individual requiring any information about the services provided by the Railway Executive should apply to the District Passenger Superintendent, British Railways, Leeds, or any station master.

---

**SCARBOROUGH 9/-**
**TUESDAY, AUGUST 25th**

Cleckheaton (Spen) .......... 11 38 a.m.
Liversedge (Spen) ............ 11 33 a.m.
Heckmondwike (Spen) ..... 11.30 a.m.
Return 8 55 p.m.

**BELLE VUE**
**WEDNESDAY AUGUST 26th**

Cleckheaton (Spen) .... 12.20 p.m.—6/9
Liversedge (Spen) ...... 12.25 p.m.—5/9
Heckmondwike (Spen) .. 12.29 p.m.—5/6
Return 8.30 p.m.

**SOUTHPORT** ............. **8/6**
**MANCHESTER** ............. **5/3**
**THURSDAY, AUGUST 27th**

Cleckheaton (Spen) ........ 11. 9 a.m.
Liversedge (Spen) .......... 11.12 a.m.
Heckmondwike (Spen) ..... 11.14 a.m.
Return from Southport 8.6 p.m.
Manchester 8.56 p.m.

---

The Railway Executive published notices of closure in various editions of the local press. This notice for Cleckheaton Spen station appeared on 21st November, 1952 and notices for the other five stations were published on 11th September, 1953.

A selection of holiday excursion trains for 1953 is shown, these used Cleckheaton Spen station eight months after it was officially closed.

departure to Leeds only having one regular passenger who paid 11½d. for a third class return.

The station buildings were not demolished immediately and some excursion and holiday trains stopped there during August and September to cater for the local holiday weeks.

The goods yard did remain open for freight traffic which was mainly coal distribution by local merchants.

A more cheerful event in 1951 was the entry by the station master, Mr D. Clegg, of Gomersal in the best kept station competition for the Wakefield area of the North Eastern Region.

The railway workers of Gomersal spent many weeks during the summer months preparing the station. White paint and flowers were the main theme with all the dull parts being painted, and the station drive and forecourt surround planted with shrubs, flowers and a rockery.

The competition was judged in August by the district operating superintendent, Mr C. Birch, whose job was difficult because of the high standard of tidiness and cleanliness. In a close run thing, Gomersal was awarded 4th prize, the other winners being Pontefract Tanshelf (1st prize), Northorpe North Road (2nd prize), Rawcliffe (3rd prize) and Crigglestone (5th prize).

A formal notice of closure for Cleckheaton Spen station appeared in local newspapers on 21st November, 1952. This announcement did not appear to rouse much action from the local public.

The station was very inconveniently sited, when compared with the Central station, and was only served by a very infrequent service, being confined mainly to workmen's peak periods during the early morning and tea time. Less than ten people a day used the station and receipts had dropped to about £20 per month. The only time that the station really took any money was at holiday times, when special long distance and excursion trains were run.

Goods activity also must have been poor because the goods agent, Mr T. Hartley, was in charge of both Cleckheaton Spen and Central locations. The latter had a far more healthy goods trade, being on the more conveniently located ex-L&Y line to Bradford, Huddersfield and, more importantly, Wakefield, which meant a direct link with the large marshalling yard at Healey Mills.

As there was no Sunday service the station closed after the last train on Saturday 3rd January, 1953. Some excursion trains stopped throughout the summer of 1953 and to cater for the local holiday weeks in late August and early September.

During April 1953 considerable feeling was expressed in the Mirfield district against the proposal of the Railway Executive to close Northorpe Higher and Battyeford stations. Petitions protesting against the closure were organised, and, at a meeting of the Mirfield council, it was decided to inform the Railway Executive that in the opinion of the council the existing facilities at Northorpe and Battyeford should be retained. The council said that in their opinion the reason for the decrease in passenger traffic was due to the very infrequent service on the line. They suggested that the Railway Executive should give serious consideration to the introduction of a railcar service

These two rather poor quality photographs have been included as they show two rare views of steam locomotives at Heckmondwike. *(Above)* Stanier '8F' No. 48104 on an engineering train in 1957.  *Author*

*(Below)* A standard class '9F' descends the newly laid spur in April 1966 whilst in the background is the chemical works of J.C. Oxley. The ex-L&Y Ravensthorpe branch is to the right.  *G.B. Goldthorp*

running at a much greater frequency. It was also agreed to ask neighbouring local authorities to join a protest to the Railway Executive over the possible closure of stations in their area.

An intimation from the district passenger superintendent of the North Eastern Region, that consideration was being given to the question of closing Liversedge Spen and Gomersal stations to passenger traffic, was considered by Spenborough Council. The committee recommended that the matter be deferred, in order to instruct the clerk to ascertain particulars of traffic at the stations during the last year, and to obtain the views of the Spen Valley Trades Council on the proposal.

Heckmondwike Urban District Council were approached by British Railways for their views on a proposal to close the Spen station to passenger traffic and the matter came before a meeting of the general works committee on Monday 4th May.

By Friday 15th May there was a unanimous protest by local trades councils against the proposed closing of the stations at Battyeford, Northorpe Higher, Heckmondwike Spen, Liversedge Spen and Gomersal. Following a statement by the Transport Users Consultative Committee (TUCC) for the Yorkshire area, however, it was decided that there were insufficient grounds to oppose the station closures. The decision not to oppose the closures was made after enquiries revealed a very unfavourable financial state of affairs.

British Railways made a formal announcement and a notice of closure appeared in local newspapers on 11th September.

Mirfield council had decided to approach their MP for his support and they hoped to have that of Heckmondwike and Spenborough councils, but this did not seem to be forthcoming.

Mr G. Smith, station master at Heckmondwike said he understood that the infrequent service was not much better before the war but, according to the number of tickets collected during the past year, about 12,500 people had arrived at the Spen station.

Saturday October 3rd was the last day of stopping services, and the stations experienced far more than their usual number of passengers. People started to gather on the platform of Heckmondwike station more than one hour before the last train to Leeds was due to arrive. This train departed Huddersfield from platform 1 in the ordinary way with no special ceremony at 10.33 pm. It was a "Saturday only" train calling at all stations to Leeds via Heckmondwike. Among the party waiting at Heckmondwike was Mr Walter Collett aged 70 years and his brother Norman aged 66 years, both of whom had travelled on the first day of passenger services over the line in 1900.

As the train emerged from the tunnel to enter the station the people waiting on the platform struck up with a chorus of "Auld Lang Syne". The local newspaper was there to take a photograph of the party and make a note of the final comments of interested passengers. Amid the clattering of carriage doors and the hissing of steam from the locomotive, the last stopping train to Leeds made a noisy departure, thanks to exploding fog detonators which had been placed on the line to signal its farewell. The train was on its last uphill journey to Liversedge Spen; the fare was 3d.

The site of Heckmondwike Spen station nine years after its closure in June 1962 showing the distant signal for Liversedge as a lower quadrant. *Peter E. Baughan*

By 20th May, 1965 the signal had been resited to the centre of the platform as an upper quadrant semaphore; the 3 pm Liverpool to Newcastle service hauled by an English Electric Type 4 emerges from the tunnel. *G.B. Goldthorp*

## AFTER NATIONALIZATION

On arrival at Liversedge Spen the party was met by leading porter Mr E. Rawnsley, who had worked on the line for 39 years graduating from junior porter. During his last few years at Liversedge Spen Mr Rawnsley virtually ran the station single-handed. The last train departed for Leeds at 10.55 pm and everyone crossed over to the other platform to wait for the last train to Huddersfield. At Liversedge Spen passengers wishing to cross from one platform to the other had to walk down to street level, along Listing Lane under the railway bridge and enter the station from the other side.

The train arrived a few minutes late and departed amidst scenes of farewell; after closing the station for the last time Mr Rawnsley and Mr G.E. Noble, who had 25 years service, were transferred to other stations in the area.

The train made light work of the short downhill journey to Heckmondwike, where the party were again met by station master Smith who said there had been numerous requests for tickets issued on the last day, presumably by collectors. A green light from the guard to the driver of locomotive No. 41257, a blast on the whistle and the 11.26 pm "Saturdays only" to Huddersfield departed eight minutes late; the red tail lamp disappearing into Heckmondwike tunnel. As this train did not stop at Northorpe Higher and Battyeford, the stopping service on the Heaton Lodge and Wortley line was no more, the gas lights were extinguished and the station closed its doors after 53 years of service.

Locomotive No. 41257 was one of six, Nos. 41254–41259, which were shedded at Farnley Junction during this period. These were light mixed traffic locomotives introduced by the LMS in 1946 for short-haul stopping services. There were 130 built, some after nationalization, and they were quite nippy provided they were not overloaded, but they handled the three coaches of these local stopping trains quite easily.

After the passenger stations had closed, the line up the Spen Valley was administered by the appropriate station master for each section of the ex-L&Y central line. For example the station master at Cleckheaton was based at Cleckheaton Central but also looked after Cleckheaton Spen and a similar arrangement applied at Heckmondwike.

The mid-1950s saw the remaining houses in Walkley Bottoms disappear in a slum clearance programme, and later the Urban District Council used about half the site as a refuse tip, bringing it level with the ex-L&Y Mirfield and Ravensthorpe branches. The level crossing was the only suitable access to the site so it must have seen more use during this period than at any other time during its existence.

A particular feature of railway embankments in the 1940s and 1950s was their use as allotment gardens, to "dig for victory" during the war. My father had an allotment garden on the embankment at Heckmondwike, although my memory of it was that it was not successful because of a large colony of ants which did not take kindly to having their home dug up. Embankments also attracted boys wanting to build dens; one day the station master, Mr D. Bunce, caught us and we got a strong "telling off" for trespassing.

The remainder of the 1950s saw the Heaton Lodge and Wortley line used mainly for freight workings, these were at their heaviest during the night

Two views of Stanier "Jubilee" class No. 45581 *Bihar and Orissa* passing Birstall Town goods yard and signal box with the 11 am Leeds to Manchester express on 30th June, 1962. *(Both) Peter E. Baughan*

Birstall goods yard looking towards Leeds; the warehouse was a similar design to the one at Gildersome and coal merchants were still working from here in 1962.
*Peter E. Baughan*

The same view taken in 1986 shows how the scene has changed with the only railway item to survive being the loading gauge post. *Author*

with very little traffic during the daytime. The pick-up goods still came to shunt the yard at Heckmondwike two or three times a week, and always in the mornings. Travelling in the direction of Huddersfield to Leeds, it was usually hauled by a WD '8F' "Austerity" but on one occasion I saw it hauled by a very unusual visitor, "Patriot" class No. 45538 *Giggleswick*. The main reason for the pick-up calling at Heckmondwike, was the tanker delivery service to the National Benzole distribution depot at J.C. Oxleys chemical works in Walkley Lane. Most businesses used the ex-L&Y Central line goods depot at Heckmondwike, but, on occasions, traders used the Spen line goods yard, so the rust did get rubbed off the rails periodically. The company known as Processed Fibres seemed to be the main user of the yard, with large bales of what appeared to be jute.

Two or three non stop passenger services used the line during the early evenings, and were interspersed with one or two freight workings. The passing times at Heckmondwike were:

| | |
|---|---|
| 4.55 pm to Leeds – | Express passenger, always hauled by a Stanier '5MT' "Black Five". |
| 6.00 pm to Leeds – | Very fast freight, always hauled by a "Black Five" it usually consisted of one or two closed vans and a brake van, occasionally only a locomotive and brake van but it still travelled fast. |
| 6.30 pm to Leeds – | Local passenger service hauled by a '4MT' tank locomotive of the Fowler or Stanier variety, sometimes a '2MT' Ivatt tank locomotive hauling three carriages of the non-corridor type. |
| 6.55 pm to Leeds – | This was the premier train of the line, being a Liverpool Lime Street to Newcastle express and always double headed. The usual train locomotive, Monday to Saturday, was a "Jubilee" class with locomotives 45558 *Manitoba*, 45559 *British Columbia*, 45645 *Collingwood* and 45668 *Madden* the main contenders for this working. At the time all these locomotives were shedded at Patricroft (10C). The pilot locomotive Monday to Friday was usually a Stanier "Black Five" with occasionally a Hughes/Fowler "Crab" being substituted. On Saturdays we used to wait with excitement because the pilot locomotive would be either a "Patriot" class or a "Royal Scot" class. Watching this train for the first time on a Saturday, the pilot locomotive was "Patriot" class No. 45539 *E.C. Trench* and the train locomotive was "Jubilee" class 45559 *British Columbia*. I was eight years old at the time and the sight of this train pounding through the cutting at Heckmondwike well and truly put railways in my blood. |
| 7.45 pm to Leeds – | Express passenger hauled by a "Black Five" or a BR Standard '5MT'. |
| 7.45 pm to Huddersfield – | Slow freight and almost without exception hauled by a WD '8F' "Austerity". |

The GNR Dewsbury to Bradford line passes above the Heaton Lodge & Wortley line at Howden Clough, Birstall. The Birstall distant signal can be seen at the far end of the cutting.  *Peter E. Baughan*

A more recent photograph at the site of Upper Birstal Station showing the passenger subway tunnel (now bricked up) halfway up the wall.  *Author*

The south portal of Gildersome Tunnel. *V.R. Anderson*

Stanier "Jubilee" class No. 45695 *Minotaur* passes under Nab Lane bridge at Howden Clough, Birstall with the 3.25 pm Manchester to Newcastle express, on 2nd September, 1961. *D. Holmes*

Gildersome goods yard looks a desolate place on 30th June, 1962, reduced to a single siding being used to store condemned coaching stock. The small part of the building with the brick chimney would originally be used as the warehouse office, and a telephone must have been installed as there are insulators on the corner of the large building. *(Both) Peter E. Baughan*

8.45 pm to Huddersfield – This slow freight could be hauled by almost anything such as a Stanier '8F', LNW '7F' 'G2' class or a WD '8F' "Austerity".

There was one other regular train which ran Saturday only.
3.00 pm to Huddersfield – Express passenger hauled by a "Jubilee" class. It also seemed to carry a number of troops among its passengers.

During the daylight hours in the summer months we used to watch these trains from various locations. The top of the embankment in Horton or Brunswick Street, the site of the old station or opposite the Old Hall in Cook Lane, where the catch point could be watched clicking away as the wheels ran through, but my favourite place was at the level crossing of the ex-L & Y railway in Walkley Bottoms. From this vantage point trains could be watched thundering over the steel viaduct, especially the 6.55 pm double-header.

Heckmondwike Spen signal box was sited at the goods yard in Walkley Lane; in LNWR days it was named Heckmondwike Goods because there used to be another box named Heckmondwike Station. The Spen signal box was quite small and worked on a one shift system, it was manned from early morning until just after midday when the box was switched out and all signals set to "clear" until next day. Most of the signals were upper quadrant semaphore being of more modern LMS or BR type, but both distants and the starting signal for Leeds, which was directly opposite the signal box, were an older lower quadrant semaphore.

During the early 1960s a certain amount of re-signalling took place over the line, resiting some signals into more favourable positions and all the lower quadrant semaphores were replaced with more modern upper quadrant signals.

On Sundays there were no trains except when the line was used as a diversion due to engineering work on the Leeds and Huddersfield line (via Dewsbury), or when engineering work was taking place on the Heaton Lodge and Wortley line itself.

My big regret regarding this period of time through the 1950s was not having the foresight to make a photographic record.

On Wednesday 11th July, 1962, after darkness had fallen, a thunderstorm swept the Spen Valley. The thunder and lightning disturbed a herd of 31 young bullocks and heifers which were grazing in a field beside the railway in the vicinity of the south end of Gomersal tunnel. The panic-stricken herd stampeded through an allegedly broken railway fence, and wandered along the track towards Cleckheaton.

Eventually the herd of cattle was met by a train, unfortunately it happened to be a Swansea to York express travelling at speed, which ploughed through the herd killing eight bullocks and six heifers. When the driver managed to stop the train, one of the beasts was found to be stuck under the front of the locomotive. The train was held up for about one hour while some slaughter men were called to the scene to remove the carcass from the locomotive. Meanwhile Mr Hirst, the owner of the cattle, had the task of rounding up the survivors. No persons were injured and the locomotive only suffered minor

English Electric Type 4 No. D235 *Apapa*, one of the new breed of diesel electric locomotives which were rapidly taking over many of the passenger services during the early 1960s. Photographed on 30th June, 1962 descending the flying junction at Farnley, and later to be renumbered as BR class 40 No. 40035, it was withdrawn from revenue earning service during August 1984 and cut up for scrap by BR at Crewe Works during June 1985.
*Peter E. Baughan*

The 5 pm Liverpool to Newcastle double-headed express descends the flying junction at Farnley on 15th August, 1960, being hauled by two "Jubilee" class locomotives, No. 45581 *Bihar and Orissa* piloting No. 45663 *Jervis*.
*D. Holmes*

damage. After the express had left, the job of clearing all the carcasses from the railway took most of the night and it was necessary to divert some freight trains via Dewsbury, but no other passenger trains were affected.

Upon investigation to find how the cattle had got onto the line, the railway inspectors thought that they had squeezed through a stile which was too narrow for fully grown animals, but Mr Hirst disagreed, saying he had reported the fencing broken in several places on a number of occasions.

In the early 1960s the line still saw quite a number of services, freight during the night and express passenger trains during the daytime. These were part of the Liverpool to Newcastle and York to Swansea services, with additional holiday services during the summer months. The Liverpool to Hull "Trans Pennine" dmu service also commenced running over the line on 2nd January, 1961 with services which did not require to stop at Dewsbury.

Before the Beeching era, most of the goods yards along this line were used for stabling sets of coaches which were only used on "Specials" to the coast, or football matches at weekends. These coaches were appreciated by people who were sleeping rough and by local boys and girls for courting. They were also a target for thieves, as some sets stabled at Cleckheaton in 1962 were stripped of all their brass fittings, the theft not being noticed until British Railways came to use the coaches.

Dr Beeching was appointed Chairman of the British Transport Commission on 1st June, 1961. In his report of the 27th March, 1963 he advocated the closure of more than 2,000 stations and numerous branch lines. Before Dr Beeching left the (by then) British Railways Board in 1965, he had also proposed the closure of some main lines, notably the east coast main line north of Newcastle. Thankfully these proposals were rejected.

The passenger stations on this line had already closed but with British Railways operating at a considerable loss, this spelled doom for many other lines and the Heaton Lodge and Wortley was no exception. As a step towards eliminating this duplicate route, all but one of the express services were diverted on 7th September, 1964 to the alternative route via Dewsbury. The only passenger train now running over the line was the 3 pm Liverpool Lime Street to Newcastle service, which left Huddersfield at 4.33 pm, entered the line at Spen Valley Junction at 4.39 pm and left the line at Farnley Junction at 4.58 pm, arriving Leeds City at 5.03 pm.

During the last week of October, British Railways issued a public notice announcing their intention to divert this last remaining passenger service. Four objections were received from individuals but one of these proved to be fictitious. After gathering all the relative information from the three objectors, the TUCC decided there was very little or no weight in the objections and agreed that the service be diverted.

From August 1965 the line between Farnley Junction and Liversedge Spen was abandoned, the track was lifted, together with the removal of most of the steel bridges. British Railways estimated a saving of £40,800 associated with track and signal maintenance and renewal.

The line from Liversedge Spen to Spen Valley Junction was retained, because British Railways had to supply the fuel oil terminal of Charrington Hargreaves, which was at the former Liversedge Spen goods yard. This

(*Above*) At 7 am on the morning of 27th June, 1985, No. 47 308 arrives with a delivery to Hargreaves Fuel Oils Ltd, Liversedge. Track facilities here do not make it easy for a collection of empty tanks to be made at the same time as a delivery so the locomotive usually runs light engine in either direction to or from Healey Mills, as shown *below*.

On 1st April, 1985 No. 47 303 returned to Healey Mills having just passed under Brunswick Street bridge; the locomotive is travelling through Heckmondwike cutting.
(*Both*) Author

company built the terminal in 1963 and today is known as Hargreaves Fuel Oils Ltd. The terminal is equipped with two parallel sidings for unloading rail tanks.

The first train of fuel oil arrived from the Mobil Oil Company terminal at Ellesmere Port, Cheshire on Tuesday 26th November, 1963. Each tank wagon had a capacity of 27 tons and carried 6,500 gallons of fuel oil.

After the Heaton Lodge and Wortley line had closed, British Railways were in the position of having to provide a delivery service to Liversedge, which in railway terms was a very isolated location. This was overcome to some extent in 1966, when a new rail connection was laid through Heckmondwike Spen goods yard to connect with the ex-L&Y Ravensthorpe branch. This enabled the original route from Spen Valley Junction to Heckmondwike Spen to be closed, after which the short stretch of line up to Liversedge was really a branch of the ex-L&Y line from Healey Mills to Low Moor. The Ravensthorpe branch itself was under threat of closure, so for many years now Liversedge has been served by a single track route from the Calder Valley line at Thornhill.

Liversedge Spen goods yard was sold to Hargreaves in 1967, after the other traders operating from the goods yard had vacated the site.

This saga has now come full circle with the terminal being put into "mothballs" during August 1986, the company saying that due to the decline of local industry it was no longer economical to have a terminal in the industrial West Riding.

Since closure of the through line in 1965 the only passenger train to visit Liversedge was an enthusiasts special on Saturday 16th May, 1981 named "The Doncaster Rover". The special, which was organised by the Lancashire Locomotive Society, visited a number of freight-only lines on its journey from Preston to Cleethorpes. The organisers had originally asked to travel over the ex-L&Y line through the Spen Valley to Low Moor but British Rail had recently closed that line to all traffic. Even so, the journey to Liversedge seemed to be enjoyed by more than 300 enthusiasts, who were hauled by English Electric class 40 No. 40 094.

All that remains of the original Heaton Lodge & Wortley line to survive as a main line is a short stretch at Heaton Lodge. In 1970 British Rail connected the Heaton Lodge and Wortley line to the Calder Valley line with a new junction named Heaton Lodge North Junction, at a point where the two lines are at the same elevation and running parallel with each other. This was done to eliminate the double crossover when the manual signal boxes were closed down and the area changed over to automatic signalling, controlled from Healey Mills power box. From 26th April, 1970 all trains from Huddersfield to Leeds now use the underpass built by the LNWR in 1896/7 and Spen Valley Junction received another new title, namely Heaton Lodge South Junction. During April 1988 both Heaton Lodge North and South Junctions have again been remodelled to incorporate a high speed layout at a cost of £600,000.

It is now more than 20 years since the line was closed and dismantled, and, apart from the short stretch at Liversedge and Heckmondwike, not

Passengers once more in Heckmondwike cutting on 16th May, 1981 as "the Doncaster Rover" heads for Liversedge behind class 40 No. 40094. The locomotive was almost at the end of its useful life being withdrawn from service during October 1982 and cut up for scrap by BR at Doncaster Works during August 1985.  *D.A. Peel*

The east portal of Gomersal tunnel as it looks today. The wall is still painted white where the signal was fixed, but large areas of the surrounding walls are host to various forms of plant life, which also partially cover the date.  *Author*

much remains today due to new developments and landscaping. All the goods yards along the old route have been sold off for various uses, both industrial and residential. The last one to be sold was the remains of Heckmondwike Spen, which was purchased in August 1984 by James Wilby Ltd, coal merchants of Dewsbury, to be used as a depot for solid fuel storage and warehousing.

During the course of my research it has given me much pleasure retracing the old route. I feel that, had the line managed to survive, it would have been an asset to the commuters of the Spen Valley and Birstall areas giving them a direct route to the city of Leeds.

There is now a different pattern to the way people commute to their employment and, as I said at the beginning, this is "progress". I wonder!

Long shadows may well fall as this really is the end of the line: the present day facilities provided at Liversedge to enable the locomotive to run round its train of empty tanks after being drawn clear of Hargreaves sidings. *Author*

# Appendix
## Working Arrangements

Although the primary function of the line was to carry the ever-increasing numbers of LNWR freight trains between Huddersfield and Leeds, the line was also a passenger carrying line and was operated under the Absolute Block System.

Signal boxes were sited at all the goods yard along the line with two boxes at Cleckheaton and one at Heckmondwike station, all controlling cross-over roads in addition to the usual signals and sidings pointwork.

*Battyeford Down Line*
A mechanical gong was fixed on the down side of the line 250 yds on the Leeds side of the points leading to the refuge siding. The method of working was that when a train had to be shunted from the down main line to the refuge siding, the guard or brakesman must first, if necessary, use the gong to signal to the driver to move forward clear of the points leading to the siding and after the points were correctly set, signal again, by means of the gong, to the driver to set back.

*Battyeford Up Line*
The heavily graded nature of the New Line meant that freight train locomotives needed to take water at Huddersfield station, the only watering place on this route between Leeds and Diggle. To counter this problem a "parachute" water column was installed at Battyeford in October 1902 at a cost of £180 and the following rule introduced: "Drivers of freight trains from Copley Hill over the New Line requiring water before reaching Diggle must take it at the water column at Battyeford, and must not stop out of course for water at Huddersfield station. The driver must signal his intention to stop for water to the signalman with one long and three short whistles."

*Heckmondwike Goods Down Line*
"When all signals are taken off, drivers of down through freight trains must not shut off steam and guards must apply their brake when the brake van is midway between the Heckmondwike Goods distant and the home signals, and must release it when the brake van is passing under the bridge immediately beyond that signal box."

*Heckmondwike Goods Up Line*
"Immediately the Heckmondwike Goods up distant signal is seen to be off, drivers of through freight trains must keep their handbrake slightly on, and the guard must release his van brake and leave the control of the train to the driver who must not apply steam until the train is passing over bridge No. 21 on the Northorpe side of Heckmondwike Goods signal box."

*Cleckheaton Down Line*
Freight trains requiring to set back into the refuge siding or goods yard from No. 2 signal box were out of view of the signalman. Communication between the signalman and the driver was established by a mechanical gong which was worked from a lever inside No. 2 box.

The code was:
1 gong – Go forward, your train is not clear of points
2 gongs – Stop
3 gongs – You may set back into siding

*Gomersal Up Line*
"Wagons must not be placed on the up main line to allow the locomotive to run round, when detaching at this place the wagons must be placed in the siding for this operation to be carried out. If there are more than seven wagons to be detached the operation must be repeated according to the number of wagons to be detached."

## THE LEEDS NEW LINE

*Gildersome Down Line*
"Down freight trains having wagons to attach or detach at Gildersome must be shunted over the points on the up line and the points set for the siding. If any train is unable to set back on the up line, wagons for this place must be taken to Copley Hill and worked back by the first available service."
   A treadle gong was fitted in Gildersome tunnel 50 yds on the Huddersfield side of the down distant signal for Gildersome and 710 yds from the Farnley Junction end of the tunnel, to give warning of the signal.

### WHISTLES

*Heckmondwike Junction*
"All locomotives passing Heckmondwike Junction on both North and South lines to and from the Heckmondwike line must give three short whistles."

*Gildersome*
"Drivers of all down trains when passing Gildersome signal box must give the following whistles:
   For COPLEY HILL ............................................................................. 1 crow
   For LEEDS ........................................................................................ 2 crows
   For FARNLEY JUNCTION LOCO. SHED ...................................... 4 short

### SPEED RESTRICTIONS

*Up Line*
   Farnley Junction to Heckmondwike Junction                          45 mph

*Down Line*
   Between 3¾ and 4 mile posts at Heckmondwike                     45 mph
   Upper Birstal to 13 mile post at Farnley                                 45 mph
   13 mile post to Farnley Junction                                            25 mph

*Heckmondwike Junction*
   Through the junction in all directions                                    20 mph

*Farnley Junction*
   Through the junction in all directions                                    25 mph

   During later years other sections of the line not mentioned above had a maximum permitted speed of                                               50 mph

### STATION INFORMATION

| | | | |
|---|---|---|---|
| Battyeford & Mirfield | ☆ | † | ▲ |
| Northorpe | | | |
| Heckmondwike | ☆ | † | ▲ |
| Liversedge | | | ▲ |
| Cleckheaton | ☆ | † | ▲ |
| Gomersal | | | ▲ |
| Upper Birstal | | | |
| Gildersome | | † | ▲ |

   ☆  *Horses can be loaded and unloaded.*
   †  *Carriages can be loaded and unloaded.*
   ▲  *Passengers' luggage is delivered.*

   "All horse boxes and carriage trucks to be detached from down trains at Battyeford & Mirfield must in all cases be marshalled next to the locomotive."

## WORKING ARRANGEMENTS

### PASSENGER WORKINGS

Maximum number of vehicles on passenger trains with one engine

| Type of engine | From Leeds | From Huddersfield |
|---|---|---|
| 4 ft 6 in. Passenger side tank | Equal to 7 | Equal to 8 |
| 5 ft 6 in. Passenger side tank | Equal to 8 | Equal to 9 |
| Six wheeled coupled 'DX' engine | Equal to 9 | Equal to 10 |
| 18 in. cylinder engine | Equal to 10 | Equal to 11 |

"The maximum load for two engines in either direction is equal to 17 vehicles."

### FREIGHT WORKINGS

*Loading of Goods and Mineral Trains*

| Place | 'DX' or Tank engine Minerals | Goods | Empties | 18 in.cylinder or coal engine Minerals | Goods | Empties | 3 cylinder compound Minerals | Goods | Empties | 4 cylinder compound Minerals | Goods | Empties |
|---|---|---|---|---|---|---|---|---|---|---|---|---|
| | Maximum number of wagons allowed ||||||||||||
| Huddersfield to Cleckheaton | 18 | 27 | 40 | 21 | 32 | 47 | 30 | 40 | 60 | 35 | 50 | 60 |
| Cleckheaton to Leeds | 16 | 24 | 35 | 19 | 28 | 40 | 24 | 36 | 55 | 28 | 42 | 60 |
| Leeds to Cleckheaton* | 16 | 24 | 36 | 19 | 35 | 45 | 24 | 45 | 60 | 28 | 50 | 60 |
| Cleckheaton to Huddersfield | 20 | 30 | 45 | 23 | 35 | 50 | 30 | 45 | 60 | 35 | 50 | 60 |

* "All up goods and mineral trains working over the New Line which exceed 24 loads of goods including the 20T brake vans, must be banked to Upper Birstal with the Bank Engine in the rear. The Bank Engine must not be hooked on."

By 1910 the limits had been amended to tons instead of by numbers of wagons.

| | 'DX engine Mineral Goods including BV | 18 in. cylinder or coal engine Mineral Goods including BV | 4 cyl. compound 8 wheel coupled 19 in. cyl. engine Mineral Goods including BV | Maximum Number of wagons including Brake Van |
|---|---|---|---|---|
| | Weight limit in tons ||||
| Huddersfield to Cleckheaton | 270 | 270 | 330 | 320 | 525 | 500 | 60 |
| Cleckheaton to Leeds | 240 | 240 | 285 | 280 | 420 | 420 | 60 |
| Leeds to Cleckheaton | 240 | 240 | 285 | 280 | 510 | 420 | 60 |
| Cleckheaton to Huddersfield | 360 | 300 | 300 | 350 | 525 | 500 | 60 |

"From Saturday midnight to Sunday midnight, down goods and mineral trains, when worked by a large engine, may be made up to equal 69 loads of goods and a 20T Brake Van between Huddersfield Hillhouse and Copley Hill via the New Line."

List of refuge sidings and intervals to be observed in despatching goods and mineral trains in advance of fast passenger trains to and from such sidings:

## Down Trains – Refuge Sidings Huddersfield to Leeds

| Distance | | From | To | Length of Siding in yds | No. of Wagons Siding Estimated to hold | Margins for Express Trains with limited loads – Running Through | Margins for Express Trains with limited loads – From Rest | Margins for Trains with full loads – Running Through | Margins for Trains with full loads – From Rest | Note |
|---|---|---|---|---|---|---|---|---|---|---|
| m. | yds | | | | | | | | | |
| 3 | 1105 | Hillhouse Yard | Eattyeford & Mirfield | 367 | 60 | 8 mins | 10 mins | 10 mins | 12 mins | |
| 2 | 938 | Battyeford & Mirfield | Heckmondwike Goods | 310 | 50 | 8 mins | 10 mins | 10 mins | 12 mins | A |
| 1 | 150 | Heckmondwike Goods | Liversedge | 265 | 40 | 5 mins | 8 mins | 8 mins | 10 mins | |
| 1 | 788 | Liversedge | Cleckheaton | 480 | 70 | 5 mins | 8 mins | 8 mins | 10 mins | |
| 1 | 710 | Cleckheaton | Upper Birstal | 290 | 40 | 10 mins | 12 mins | 12 mins | 15 mins | B |
| 4 | 1096 | Upper Birstal | Farnley Junction | – | – | 10 mins | 12 mins | 12 mins | 15 mins | C |

Notes:
A.  Trains having work to do at Northorpe must have a 20 minutes margin
B.  Trains having work to do at Gomersal must have a 30 minute margin
C.  Trains having work to do at Gildersome must have a 20 minute margin

## Up Trains – Refuge Sidings Leeds to Huddersfield

| Distance | | From | To | Length of Siding in yds | No. of Wagons Siding Estimated to hold | Margins for Express Trains with limited loads – Running Through | Margins for Express Trains with limited loads – From Rest | Margins for Trains with full loads – Running Through | Margins for Trains with full loads – From Rest | Note |
|---|---|---|---|---|---|---|---|---|---|---|
| m. | yds | | | | | | | | | |
| 1 | 1603 | Farnley Junction | Gildersome | 280 | 40 | 8 mins | 10 mins | 10 mins | 12 mins | D |
| 2 | 1577 | Gildersome | Upper Birstal | 320 | 50 | 15 mins | 18 mins | 18 mins | 23 mins | |
| 2 | 577 | Upper Birstal | Cleckheaton | 230 | 33 | 6 mins | 8 mins | 8 mins | 10 mins | E |
| 1 | 972 | Cleckheaton | Liversedge | 420 | 60 | 5 mins | 7 mins | 7 mins | 10 mins | |
| 1 | 51 | Liversedge | Heckmondwike Goods | 227 | 33 | 5 mins | 7 mins | 7 mins | 10 mins | |
| 2 | 1101 | Heckmondwike Goods | Battyeford & Mirfield | 204 | 30 | 8 mins | 10 mins | 10 mins | 12 mins | F |
| 2 | 765 | Battyeford & Mirfield | Kirkburton Junction | 400 | 60 | 10 mins | 12 mins | 12 mins | 15 mins | |

Notes:
D.  Trains having work to do at Gildersome must have a 15 minutes margin
E.  Trains having work to do at Gomersal must have a 15 minute margin
F.  Trains having work to do at Northorpe must have a 20 minute margin